450
1

D1095309

# THE LOGICAL EPIC

# THE LOGICAL EPIC

## A STUDY OF THE ARGUMENT

### OF

## *PARADISE LOST*

DENNIS H. BURDEN

HARVARD UNIVERSITY PRESS

Cambridge, Massachusetts

1967

*Printed in Great Britain*

To
ELEANOR

# Preface

This book is a study of the logic of the theme of *Paradise Lost*. It is especially concerned with the constraints within which the argument is made to move. It shows how the account of the Fall is disciplined by the need to work to the best sense of the Genesis story. It argues that Milton, making *Paradise Lost* the right Christian poem, was very aware of how it could be made into the wrong unChristian poem, and that this awareness made for extensive and dynamic application.

Miss K. M. Lea, Dr A. D. S. Fowler and Mr F. W. Bateson read various earlier drafts. I should like to acknowledge the help that they gave, and to say how grateful I am to them for their patience, encouragement and criticism. Dr D. A. Rees also helped me on points of detail.

Dennis H. Burden

*Trinity College,*
*Oxford.*

# Contents

# I

# The Logic of God's Providence

WHEN, at the opening of *Paradise Lost*, Milton states that his argument is to 'assert Eternal Providence/ And justifie the wayes of God to men' (I, 25-26), he is insisting on the rationality of his subject. The simple claim leads into a complicated poem, and Milton needed to be as logical in his explanation of the divine goodness as Gulliver needed to be in his explanation to the Houyhnhnms of the nature of human vice: 'All this I was forced to define and describe by putting of Cases, and making Suppositions' (*Gulliver's Travels*, Part IV, ch. iv). The assertion of divine providence is the assertion that God's goodness, justice and mercy are not contradicted by the spectacle of the world that he has made. The poem is thus an exercise in clarification, finding system and order in what could, if wrongly taken, appear to be random and inexplicable. Light is a fully appropriate metaphor for this Christian truth, a light holy and celestial by which things can be truly seen. The assertion of God's providence involves the awareness of the two dimensions of reality, the earthly and the heavenly, requiring that doubleness of vision that looks first on the glass and then, more wisely, through it:

A man that looks on glasse,
On it may stay his eye;
Or if he pleaseth, through it passe,
And then the heav'n espie.

(Herbert, 'The Elixir')

This recognition of God's providence was commonplace and of wide application.[1] It could for example provide the rationale of history which called the past to witness to the workings of a just and beneficent God. Milton's own historical writing shows that this required varying degrees of subtlety. Some cases are child's play, as when, for example, bad men come to bad ends. Thus the account of Mempricius is, in the *History of Britain*, made to represent a simple but sensational justice: a bad king, the murderer of his brother and other nobles, he suffers a grisly but just death: 'till lastly giv'n over to unnaturall lust, in the twentith of his Reigne, hunting in a Forest, he was devowr'd by Wolves' (X, 16).[2] So too Milton read the execution of Charles I as a just answer to the King's appeal to God to punish him if he were really, in the case of the Five Members, oppressing the innocent: 'God & his judgements have not bin mock'd' (*Eikonoklastes*, V, 103). All this is of a piece with some of the historical episodes listed in the *Trinity MS.* as possible material for tragedies. But there could be more complicated cases that needed much subtler handling and an altogether Swift-like 'putting of Cases, and making Suppositions.' Thus Milton's account of Cordelia in his *History* is interesting, especially when it is set against Shakespeare's. In *King Lear* Cordelia is a victim of the raw injustice of the play, her death a gratuitous horror. But Milton's account is produced with a

---

[1] See, for example, Calvin. *Institutes of the Christian Religion*, Book I, chs. xvi–xviii. For surveys of the doctrine, see: Herschel Baker, *The Dignity of Man: Studies in the Persistence of an Idea* (Cambridge, Mass., 1947), pp. 223–235; (same author), *The Wars of Truth: Studies in the Decay of Christian Humanism in the Earlier 17th. Century* (New York and London, 1952), pp. 12–25; Hiram Haydn, *The Counter-Renaissance* (New York, 1950), pp. 131–138.

[2] References to Milton's work (apart from his English poems) are to the Columbia Edition, Volume and page.

closer eye to the 'reasonableness' of the story. He is worried about what might seem the lack of true daughterly decorum in the manner of her speech to her father, and explicates it in a way that keeps her on a right moral line. She spoke 'with a loiall sadness at her Fathers infirmity, but somthing on the sudden, harsh, and glancing rather at her Sisters, then speaking her own mind' (X, 19). The fact that she vanquished her impious sisters and their impious husbands represents the just prospering of her piety (X, 21), but her eventual suicide in prison earns a rebuke: 'impatient, and now long unexercis'd to suffer, she there, as is related, killd herself' (X, 21). Milton clearly puts the account under some pressure, presenting the facts in the light of a moral hypothesis. The most logically audacious touch in his *History* is his account of Martia, the wife of Guithelac, whose rule, after her husband's death and during her son's minority, saw the promulgation of some very creditable laws. But this phenomenon of a female law-giver hardly squares with God's ordinance in Genesis 3 : 16 that man should rule over the woman. Milton saves the case by inventing a council for Martia: 'In the minority of her Son she had the rule, and then, as may be suppos'd, brought forth these Laws, not her self, for Laws are Masculin Births, but by the advice of her sagest Counselors; and therein she might do vertuously, since it befell her to supply the nonage of her Son: else nothing more awry from the law of God and Nature, then that a Woman should give Laws to Men' (X, 26). Milton's history is characteristically deductive and logical, involving him in an improvement of his sources, for Geoffrey of Monmouth, Stow and Holinshed make no moral comments about Cordelia and have no reference to any council of Martia's.

The rigour of this last case derives from the fact that Biblical authority has some bearing upon it, and this sort of rigour is all the more necessary where the facts of the case were themselves Biblical. The Bible was Christian history and so was necessarily rational because God was rational: 'being the Rule, he cannot be Irregular; nor, being Truth it self, conceaveably

3

admit the impossible society of Error,'[3] and so any snags or difficulties that the Bible narrative provided had to be smoothed out into reason and system. This was indeed where the opportunity and skill of much Biblical commentary lay.[4] The commentary was often enough logical in essence since the concern was with the rationality of the book and with the purposes of God. The Bible had to be saved on occasion from apparent inconsistency and self-contradiction in order to save God from apparent arbitrariness and absurdity. It is characteristic that the first problem that Milton wrestles with in *Samson Agonistes* (293-325) is the problem of law, the question as to why Samson, a Nazarite and hence subject to special laws, should be prompted by God (as the Bible, Judges 14: 4, says that he was) to marry a non-Jewish wife and so to violate a law to which *all* Jews were subject. This was the sort of question that Milton found it necessary to put and not to suppress. The systematization of Biblical material could be very extensive. For example, in the Preface to *The Reason of Church-Government* Milton argues not merely that the books of the Bible are in themselves reasonable, but also that the order, the disposition of the books within the Old Testament, is reasonable too:

> *Moses* therefore the only Lawgiver that we can believe to have beene visibly taught of God, knowing how vaine it was to write lawes to men whose hearts were not first season'd with the knowledge of God and of his workes, began from the book of Genesis, as a prologue to his lawes; which *Josephus* right well hath noted. That the nation of the Jewes, reading therin the universall goodness of God to all creatures in the Creation, and his peculiar favour to them in his election of *Abraham* their ancestor, from whom they could derive so many blessings upon themselves, might be mov'd to obey sincerely by knowing so good a reason of their obedience.
>
> (III, Part I, 182)

[3] Browne, *Vulgar Errors*. (*Works*, ed. G. Keynes (London, 1960), II, 21).
[4] On the commentaries, see Arnold Williams, *The Common Expositor: an Account of the Commentaries on Genesis, 1527-1633* (Chapel Hill, 1948).

This thesis collates the several books of the Old Testament into a system in much the same way that a good play collates a set of episodes into a plot. The reference to Josephus indicates that this sort of thing was a common element in Biblical commentary, but it was also something to which Milton's mind was peculiarly suited. In *The Christian Doctrine* he recommends the close scrutiny of the divine purpose as an exercise: 'Yet even believers are not always sufficiently observant of these various operations of divine providence, until they are led to investigate the subject more deeply, and become more intimately conversant with the word of God' (XV, 89-91), and himself went about this observation and investigation with unusual intensity and perseverance. He had an almost obsessive determination to see the world in rational terms, a determination for which his blindness provided the most crucial and tragic test (his opponents, with equal logic, being ready to see it as a judicial punishment inflicted upon him by God for his part in the King's death—see *Second Defence*, VIII, 67). That the resolution of difficulty did not always come easily can be seen in that strange cry of distress in his *Commonplace Book*: 'Why does God permit evil? That the account of Reason with Virtue may be correct. For virtue is attested by evil, is illuminated and trained. As Lactantius says: that Reason and Judgment may have a field in which they may exercise themselves by choosing the things that are good and shunning the things that are evil; although even these things are not satisfactory' (XVIII, 128-129). But his public voice, especially in his poetry, asks awkward questions only in order to answer them. He shows throughout a concern with the proper focusing of experience: the heavenly dimension of reason and order is the dimension of the close of *Lycidas*, 'So *Lycidas* sunk low, but mounted high' (172); and of the Spirit's world in *Comus*, 'Above the smoak and stirr of this dim spot' (5).

The declared subject of *Paradise Lost*, since it is taken from the Bible, provides much occasion for the logical explicator, and a full understanding of the poem can only be had by recognizing the sort of thinking that it committed Milton to. The poem is based necessarily on the Genesis account,[5] and the way in which it handles the awkward problems that arise when that account has to be seen as compatible with the idea of a provident God is an organic part of its nature. An example early in Book IX reflects Milton's awareness of a problem familiar enough to the commentators. The book opens with an outline of the sad effect of Heaven's judgment:

> On the part of Heav'n
> Now alienated, distance and distaste,
> Anger and just rebuke, and judgement giv'n,
> That brought into this World a world of woe,
> Sinne and her shadow Death, and Miserie
> Deaths Harbinger . . .
>
> (IX, 8-13)

Bentley provided a moving, but puzzled note on the phrase 'Deaths Harbinger': '*Harbinger* is he, that goes before some Potentate, to provide for his Reception. How then is *Misery* the Harbinger of Death? There's manifold Misery that does not usher in Death, but invokes it in vain; besides, there is Misery after Death'[6] and emended it to '*Malady*/Death's Harbinger.' Pearce did not agree that the phrase was meaningless and argued that by misery Milton meant the misery of death and disease, instancing in support the hospital scene in Book XI.[7] Bentley and Pearce thus agree about what the phrase means, and disagree merely about its good sense. But they are using the wrong sort of thinking about the phrase. The proposition that misery is Death's harbinger is not a proposition directly derived from the analysis of experience. The real point

[5] Biblical quotations are from the Authorized Version. Though Milton had access to other versions and concordances, he used chiefly the A.V. (See Harris F. Fletcher, 'The Use of the Bible in Milton's Prose,' *University of Illinois Studies in Language and Literature*, Vol. XIV, No. 3 (1929).) A very useful account of the Biblical element in Milton's poetry can be found in James H. Sims, *The Bible in Milton's Epics* (Gainsville, 1962).

[6] Ed. *Paradise Lost* (1732), p. 266.

[7] Pearce, *Review of the Text of the Twelve Books of Milton's Paradise Lost* (1733), p.291.

that Milton is making is a logical one. Although God says about the forbidden Fruit '. . . in the day that thou eatest thereof thou shalt surely die' (Genesis 2:17), nevertheless when Adam and Eve do eat the fruit they do not die. But it cannot be that God was wrong or that he changed his mind, since that would impute either error or arbitrariness to God. So what Genesis says has to be accepted as being in some way or other true. This involves the making of some discrimination about the degrees or kinds of death, and Adam and Eve have necessarily to suffer some form of death when they eat the forbidden Fruit, a form of death which is a precursor of the final stage. Hence 'Miserie/Deaths Harbinger.' The Bible does not say that Adam and Eve died in any sort of way at all, so its account clearly needs to be augmented.

A similar difficulty arises with regard to the other tree in the garden, the Tree of Life. As this Tree apparently contains within its fruit the gift of eternal life, the question arises as to what would have happened if Adam, having eaten of the Tree of Knowledge and so incurring death, had gone straight to eat the fruit of the Tree of Life, so obtaining immortality and thwarting God's doom. This is clearly impossible, but in Genesis the eating of the fruit from the first Tree and God's measures to safeguard the second are rather far apart:

22 And the LORD God said, Behold, the man is become as one of us, to know good and evil: and now, lest he put forth his hand, and take also of the tree of life, and eat, and live for ever:

23 Therefore the LORD God sent him forth from the garden of Eden, to till the ground from whence he was taken.

(Genesis 3)

But there is no way by which Adam could circumvent the doom of death. His only remedy, as Book III shows, is for someone else to die in his stead. So God's speech must be ironical and sarcastic, a point which Milton's version of it makes quite clear:

Least therefore his now bolder hand
Reach also of the Tree of Life, and eat,
And live for ever, dream at least to live
For ever, to remove him I decree . . .
(XI, 93-96)

The phrase 'dream at least to live/For ever' makes the idea a
fantasy and hence rules it out.

This hard scrutiny of Biblical material, this concern for its
rationality and logic, can, when applied to the Bible's apparent
contradictions or to its manner of metaphorical writing, furnish
wit and paradox. The details provide puzzles which can be
jocularly solved. Thus, although the Bible says that God has
lamps on his altars, '5 . . . and there were seven lamps of fire
burning before the throne, which are the seven spirits of
God' (Revelation 4), this cannot be taken to imply that God
cannot see in the dark, as Milton makes clear:

Mean while th'Eternal eye, whose sight discernes
Abstrusest thoughts, from forth his holy Mount
And from within the golden Lamps that burne
Nightly before him, saw without thir light
Rebellion rising . . .

(V, 711-715)

The poem relates the lamps to the attributes of God (in this
case his omniscience) in a way that does not occur to St John,
and the phrase 'without thir light' wittily superannuates the
lamps that Revelation gave Milton authority to include. The
darkness of Milton's Heaven, 'though darkness there might
well/Seem twilight here' (VI, 4-5) is an attempt to resolve the
apparent contradictions of Revelation on the question of the
night of the celestial city since it says both that 'there shall be no
night there' (22: 5) and that the blessed 'serve him day and
night in his temple' (7: 15). The light of hell is equally awkward. Job 10: 22 calls hell: 'A land of darkness, as darkness
itself; and of the shadow of death, without any order, and
where the light is as darkness.' Revelation 9: 2 develops the

picture a bit more: 'And he opened the bottomless pit; and there arose a smoke out of the pit, as the smoke of a great furnace; and the sun and the air were darkened by reason of the smoke of the pit.' This gives a hell with smoke but no light, so, on the principle that there is no smoke without fire, the poem posits a Hell which has indeed no light but does have flame, even if it is a strange sort of flame: 'yet from those flames/No light, but only darkness visible' (I, 61-62). The oxymoron is developed out of the apparently contradictory details of the Bible. The nature of God (especially when it is accomodated to narrative) also provides occasion for this sort of thinking. God's eyes see not only objects but thoughts (V, 711); God's resting on the Seventh Day of Creation cannot mean that he was tired: 'from his work/Desisting though unwearied' (VII, 551-552). His omnipresence can also be made to sound contradictory: 'he also went/Invisible, yet staid' (VII, 588-589); 'nor vacuous the space' (VII, 168). The rationality of the concepts is saved by paradox.

## II

This necessary reasonableness of his source and theme chimed well with Milton's theory of art. His neo-classicism, with its insistence upon the reasonable disposition of the episodes within a poem and upon the self-consistency of a poem, was an advantage when he took up the argument of *Paradise Lost*. Christian philosophy and literary theory here met, and this fact has an important bearing upon the way in which the poem is organized. The neo-classic poet was committed to a work which established a poetical justice, an ending in which the perfect distribution of reward and punishment was observed, and the Christian philosopher had the same process in view because God was provident. The word 'disposition,' used to describe the proper ordering of a set of arguments or the proper ordering of the episodes of a work of art, could also be used to describe the ordering nature of God's providence:

'This appointeth unto them their kinds of working; the disposition whereof in the purity of God's own knowledge and will is rightly termed by the name of Providence.'[8] Milton in *Samson* uses 'disposition' in the Preface to refer to his own ordering of the plot, and 'disposal' (210) and 'disposition' (368) in the text for God's ordering of his world. Thus a plot which, like the plot of *Paradise Lost*, had for its theme the providence of God was bound to meet the requirements of neo-classic theory. Calvin, coming at the matter from the philosophical end, saw God's ways as constituting the perfect plot: 'he so arranges the course of his providence, as daily to declare, by the clearest manifestations, that though all are in innumerable ways the partakers of his bounty, the righteous are the special objects of his favour, the wicked and profane the special objects of his severity . . . those things which men call fortuitous events, are so many proofs of divine providence . . . conducting all things in perfect accordance with reason'[9] and Rymer, coming from the literary end, saw that an imperfect plot manifested an improvident Deity, commenting thus upon plays that did not observe poetical justice: 'this *unequal* dispensation of rewards and punishments did perplex the *wisest*, and by the *Atheist* was made a Scandal to the *Divine Providence*.'[10] Johnson's critical view of *King Lear* is determined by this neo-classic insistence upon order, and the play's deliberate brutality, its harsh refusal to provide the providentially happy ending with which it teases its audience (Edmund's repentance (V, iii, 243) being intended to arouse the hope of rescue for Lear and Cordelia) seemed an offence against art whose purpose should be to make sense out of what seemed inconsequential and irrational, and to present its material in the light of the heavenly rather than the earthly dimension.

Milton's claim for the unique rationality and morality of

---

[8] Hooker, *Of the Laws of Ecclesiastical Polity*, Book I, ch. iii (3). (*Works* (Oxford 1888), p. 210).
[9] Calvin, *Institutes* (Book I, ch. v), trans. H. Beveridge (Edinburgh, 1863), I, 56-57.
[10] *The Critical Works of Thomas Rymer*, ed. Zimansky (New Haven and London, 1956), p. 22.

his own poem is made explicitly at the opening of Book IX
where he picks a quarrel with classical epic over that issue:

> I now must change
> These Notes to Tragic; foul distrust, and breach
> Disloyal on the part of Man, revolt,
> And disobedience: On the part of Heav'n
> Now alienated, distance and distaste,
> Anger and just rebuke, and judgement giv'n,
> That brought into this World a world of woe,
> Sinne and her shadow Death, and Miserie
> Deaths Harbinger: Sad task, yet argument
> Not less but more Heroic than the wrauth
> Of stern *Achilles* on his Foe pursu'd
> Thrice Fugitive about *Troy* wall; or rage
> Of *Turnus* for *Lavinia* disespous'd,
> Or *Neptun's* ire or *Juno's*, that so long
> Perplex'd the *Greek* and *Cytherea's* Son . . .
>
> (IX, 5-19)

The passage is a characteristic exercise in close discrimination,
turning on anger. Milton had the assistance of classical critics
in his quarrel: Horace in the *Ars Poetica* (l. 121) had characterized the wrath of Achilles as something ruthless and anarchic,
and Aristotle in the *Poetics* had seen the pursuit of Hector as an
episode which, though marvellous, was nevertheless too
ridiculous to be put on the stage,[11] so that Milton's 'Thrice
Fugitive' is not without scorn. But Milton has his own points to
make. His calling the anger of Achilles 'stern' indicates that
the anger is one that intends no reconcilement. It refers to
Achilles' refusal to make a covenant with Hector before their
battle (*Iliad*, XXII) for 'stern' is used of irreconcilable opposites,
of Satan and Gabriel for instance in their confrontation in the
Garden: 'To whom with stern regard thus *Gabriel* spake'
(IV, 877); 'To which the Fiend thus answerd frowning stern'
(IV, 924). But the anger of Milton's God is not of this order.
Founded on justice, it does not render God utterly implacable

---

[11] Trans. Ingram Bywater (Oxford, 1920), p. 83.

towards Man since God's intention is ultimately reconcilement
and mercy. Milton contrives too to make a moral case against
Virgil's epic with the word 'disespous'd.' This makes Turnus's
claim to Lavinia very strong indeed, and puts some shame on
Aeneas who stole Turnus's bride and on the gods who endorsed that act. And the last lines about the anger of Cytherea
and Juno bring Milton back to his starting point of divine
anger. The anger of his own just God is importantly differentiated from the pique of lesser and various deities. Milton
significantly names neither Odysseus nor Aeneas, calling them
simply the 'Greek' and 'Cytherea's Son,' since what mattered
was not who as individuals they were or what they were
like, but simply that one was a Greek and the other the son of
Venus, these two things being a sufficient cause for their
being the objects of divine wrath. Milton thus presents the
Odyssey and the Aeneid as stories of victimization rather than of
justice. Hence his crucial word 'perplex'd,' a key word in
Paradise Lost. The true epic story will unravel perplexity and the
Christian story must necessarily of its very nature do this, as
Adam acknowledges to Michael after he has been told that
Christian story at the end of the poem:

> O sent from Heav'n,
> Enlightner of my darkness, gracious things
> Thou hast reveald, those chiefly which concerne
> Just *Abraham* and his Seed: now first I finde
> Mine eyes true op'ning, and my heart much eas'd,
> Erwhile perplext with thoughts what would becom
> Of mee and all Mankind; but now I see
> His day, in whom all Nations shall be blest. . .
>
> (XII, 270–277)

It is this enlightenment that makes the Christian poem the best
of its kind. Milton's case against classical epic is a typical piece
of literary criticism that directs its attention to the moral and
logical implications of any particular episode. A critic is
expected to systematize a poem in the same way that a com-

mentator will systematize the Bible. It was a method of reading that, in the case of Milton himself, or Rapin, or Rymer or Johnson, allowed of much subtlety of interpretation. Milton is here concerned to establish the reasonableness of God's anger. What happens when we make the wrong hypothesis about that anger is illustrated by Sin who in Book II looks at it in an unenlightened and confused way. God, she tells Death, laughs at the prospect of Satan's fighting him:

> and knowst for whom;
> For him who sits above and laughs the while
> At thee ordain'd his drudge, to execute
> What e'er his wrath, which he calls Justice, bids . . .
> (II, 730-733)

To identify God's anger with resentment and not with justice is to make the wrong hypothesis about the case. Sin, like Homer and Virgil, systematizes wrongly.

III

It is obvious that this sort of logical and self-consistent poem is possible only for a writer who has a real capacity for systematization and concern about the framework within which any particular matter is to be fitted. This capacity and concern do not show themselves in Milton's work merely in *Paradise Lost* since his early poems display much skill in the appropriate disposition of appropriate material. Indeed if we ignore the intellectual decorum which some of those poems observe, we misunderstand what is being said. For example the classical mode which many of them adopt is elegant rather than serious, rhetorical rather than strictly true. *Arcades*, no doubt reflecting its courtly elegant occasion, is written in this fashion. The establishing of the new Arcadia is the compliment which the close of the piece pays to the Countess Dowager of Derby, but the new Arcadia, for all its modern lawn at Harefield and its new Queen, is, ideologically, no different from the old.

The singers whom the Genius of the Wood says that he listens
to when everything else is asleep

> But els in deep of night when drowsines
> Hath lock't up mortal sense, then listen I
> To the celestial *Sirens* harmony,
> That sit upon the nine enfolded Sphears,
> And sing to those that hold the vital shears,
> And turn the Adamantine spindle round,
> On which the fate of gods and men is wound.
>
> (61-67)

are, as the Fates and spindle show, the Platonic sirens of
pagan poetry, but Milton knows that he is no more likely to
find the Countess Dowager of Derby listening to them than he
is, say, to find the bones of Mansus (who, being a Christian,
would be buried) in a little urn (see *Mansus*, 90). *L'Allegro* and
*Il Penseroso* are also written within this mannered literary
mode. They set up a series of delightful situations which are
enjoyed in an atmosphere of elegant, gracious learning: 'Hebe's
cheek' (*L'Allegro*, 29), 'Joves altar' (*Il Penseroso*, 48). But
neither poem necessarily takes us very close to Milton himself.
We do not have to suppose that the references to Shakespeare
and Jonson in *L'Allegro* mean that he was an habitué of the
theatres. They are merely consistent with the hypothesis that
the poem is making about shared delights of which the
theatre is a good example. In *Il Penseroso*, about more solitary
pleasures, the plays are Greek ones and so aptly enough read
and not seen. Coherence in this sort of case is more important
than fact. In the light of this it is possible for example to be
sceptical about what the early poems tell us about Milton's
early epic plans. In *At a Vacation Exercise* Milton, addressing a
college audience, talks about his projected epic, the 'graver
subject' (30), in these terms:

> Such where the deep transported mind may soare
> Above the wheeling poles, and at Heav'ns dore
> Look in, and see each blissful Deitie

How he before the thunderous throne doth lie,
Listening to what unshorn *Apollo* sings
To th'touch of golden wires, while *Hebe* brings
Immortal Nectar to her Kingly Sire . . .

(33-39)

This vision of a pagan Olympus with its plurality of gods does
not necessarily tell us anything about the epic that he really
intends one day to write. He tells his audience that he will write
a serious poem but the poem that he there outlines is the serious
poem that he would write if he were the classical poet that he is
pretending to be. He has indeed the general intention of
writing an impressive poem, but the particulars of it given
here belong to the logical consistency of *At a Vacation Exercise*
and are not necessarily actual particulars of the projected
poem. The same caution needs to be observed with regard to
Milton's supposed Arthurian epic. In *Mansus* he appears to
have the intention of writing an Arthuriad:

O, may my lot vouchsafe to me a friend so fine, one who knows
so well how to honour the men of Phoebus, true men, if ever
I shall bring back to my songs the kings of my native land, and
Arthur, who set wars in train even 'neath the earth, or shall I tell
of the high-hearted heroes bound together as comrades at that
peerless table, and—O, may the spirit come to my aid—I shall
break to pieces Saxon phalanxes under the might of Britons'
warring.

(I, Part I, 293)

But again this subject may be part of the logic of the poem.
Milton is hardly likely to tell a cultured Italian, friend of Tasso,
that he is thinking of writing a poem on something like this:
'Brightrick of west Saxons poyson'd by his wife Ethelburga
Offa's daughter who dyes miserably also in beggery after
adultery in a nunnery' (*Trinity MS.: Brit. Trag. 23*, XVIII, 243).
The Arthur reference is part of the hypothesis upon which
*Mansus* is written, that there is a real community of interest,

culture and knowledge between the poet and the person addressed. Milton certainly shows his awareness of this community in his letter to Charles Dati in 1647 admitting that the aggressive anti-Catholicism of some of his poems might displease an Italian reader (*Familiar Letters*, XII, 51). So, writing to Manso, he gives himself the conventional European epic subject. That the Arthur subject appears again in *Damon's Epitaph* (I, Part I, 313), this time related more specifically to the theme of British history in which Milton was indeed interested, may again be no more than the right sort of gesture to make towards Diodati. There is after all no reference to the Arthur story in the *Trinity MS.:* Milton's interest there is much more in Alfred, a true historical figure.

Perhaps the best case of where the systematization is as much by way of the occasion and good form as it is by way of ideology is provided by *Comus*. As befits its occasion it is not too drily moral, nor too rigorously intellectual a poem. Milton's commitment was to entertain. The Bridgewater family wanted an occasion for pleasure and compliment, Lawes an occasion for music and song to show off his paces. The moral of the poem was itself a compliment to the chastity of the Lady Alice Egerton, and it is interesting to note how Milton in the masque accommodates it to the occasion by a very careful choice of episode. The Lady's plight must be one that carries the right implications. It cannot be one that she is in because of her own moral error, nor can it be one in which she might find herself really doing the wrong thing, nor can she be in the throes of a moral struggle. For all these things would be too near to the tragic, and would be no compliment to the Lady Alice and so not welcomed by the audience for whom the masque was written. Appearing as herself, her innocence must be total and effortless and it turns out to be so impressive that it almost shames Comus himself into virtue (800-805), something that would appeal to the Earl her father. Furthermore while the family would be pleased to hear the chastity of their daughter praised, they might be embarrassed or offended to see it directly assaulted. Milton's solution here is to make the Lady's temptation sexual only by implication: when, at the crucial point, Comus places her in the enchanted chair and offers her the magic cup, the appetite appealed to is not lust but thirst. It turns out too that the cup and the chair are relevant to entirely separate issues since the Lady can of her own free will drink or not drink of the cup, but cannot of her own free will get out of the chair. That she chooses not to drink of the cup is a nice moral compliment to her. The chair on the other hand is there in order to create a situation in which the Lady, while in no way having her moral virtue impugned, is nevertheless in need of rescue. This is done to provide a role for the brothers whose saving of their sister is consequently a compliment to them. The Platonism of the masque must also be seen as part of its occasion. It offered the opportunity for the graceful and poetical presentation of a moral issue. Milton acknowledges in the *Apology for Smectymnuus* (III, Part I, 305-306) that chastity can be learned from Plato and Xenophon even though its best foundation is St Paul, and the Earl of Bridgewater might think that St Paul was somewhat too solid a foundation for what was after all a festive night. *Comus* provides a beautiful example of a poet working out the logic of an occasion.

## IV

Fineness and coherence of structure are thus characteristic of Milton's work, and in *Paradise Lost* he had committed himself to the most logical thesis possible. All the episodes of the poem had to be consistent with its central theme. Digressions and episodes were a necessary part of the epic poem, and Renaissance critics were accustomed to looking hard at them. Providing variety and delight, they nevertheless had to be developed with some care and moral responsibility. Castelvetro for example criticized Virgil's handling of the Dido episode in the *Aeneid* since it took away the very real nobility that history showed in Dido.[12] Eighteenth century editors liked to draw attention to some of the episodes in *Paradise Lost* as typical beauties of the poem, and it was recognized that the nature of Milton's subject raised particular difficulties in this respect. Addison comments that Milton 'was obliged to proceed with the greatest caution in every Thing that he added out of his own Invention,'[13] and Johnson makes the same point: 'Whoever considers the few radical positions which the Scriptures afforded him will wonder by what energetick operations he expanded them to such extent and ramified them to so much variety, restrained as he was by religious reverence from licentiousness of fiction.'[14] Milton was not of course throughout his poem committed to a mode of perfect literalness since poetry had after all a rhetorical as well as a logical basis, but he had to move carefully. This had indeed been customary with him where important issues were involved, even as early as his years in Cambridge as the *Second Prolusion* shows. The subject of the piece is the music of the spheres and, since that idea is Pythagorean and pagan, Milton starts off with some reservations before he allows himself to use it. The idea is, he explains, a fable, but it suggests the idea of cosmic harmony which is a Christian truth: 'Surely, if indeed he taught the harmony of the spheres and that the heavens revolved with melodious charm, he wished to signify by it, in his wise way, the very loving and affectionate relation of the orbs and their eternally uniform revolutions according to the fixed laws of necessity' (XII, 151). With this warrant from the poets, Milton proposes to use the same freedom of allegorical speech in the Prolusion: 'Wherefore, a few words at least suggest themselves to be pronounced, as they say, with open hand and with rhetorical embellishment, about that famous heavenly harmony, concerning which very shortly there is to be a

[12] See *Literary Criticism: Plato to Dryden*, ed. Allan H. Gilbert (New York, 1940), p. 326.
[13] *Spectator*, No. 267.
[14] *Lives of the Poets*, ed. G. Birkbeck Hill (Oxford, 1905), I, 183.

disputation with the closed fist' (XII, 149-151). The later discussion here referred to is the tougher logical disputation which was to follow. So Milton opens the Prolusion with a hard logical punch (i.e. the idea is fable), but then he unclenches his fist a bit and goes in for a rather more rhetorical and graceful development of the idea. (It is interesting and characteristic that it is developed in accordance with the pagan system adopted throughout the piece, going only as far as Pythagoras himself could have gone. Thus man's failure to hear the music any more is accounted for in purely pagan terms: his ears are closed and his happiness lost because the gods have been angered by Prometheus' theft of fire from Heaven.) *Paradise Lost* also has room for the graceful and the ornate, but Milton is concerned about the limits within which his inventions can operate and what degree of tolerance his theme allows them. His episodes have a variety of warranty. Some are in essence metaphorical representations of a truth, others are of things which might well have happened and happen not inconsistently with Milton's main scheme, others are of things which necessarily had to happen. For authority Milton can claim the Bible, logical deduction, the accommodation theory by which mysterious things are familiarized to human understanding by parable and metaphor, and sometimes classical precedent by which certain fables can be seen as shadows or remnants of a Christian truth. Thus, since Genesis says that God provided a guard to secure the Garden after the Fall, it is not unreasonable for Milton to suppose that he provided one for it before the Fall for the same reason. And he can allow his fantastic, Swift-like Limbo (III, 444-497), or take over from Homer the chain by which the world hangs (II,1051), or allow Raphael to discourse about the music of the spheres (V, 620-626), since these things image important truths about human folly, or the world's dependence upon God, or cosmic harmony. But, since it is ultimately based upon the Bible, *Paradise Lost* has for much of the time to work within very tight limits, and the fist of logic closes hard over most of the poem. Thus in the account of the creation of the world in Book VII, where he is working closely to Biblical material, Milton leaves out the Homeric chain and the music of the spheres. Indeed, perhaps glancing jocularly at the latter, he points out that when God had finished his work it was, as Job 38: 7 indicates, the stars that sang while—and this Job does not indicate—'The Planets in thir station list'ning stood' (VII, 563). The poem, being more historical and scriptural at those points, is there kept free from pagan fable.

The explicit Christian parts of the poem hence require more logical strictness and a tighter mode of working. The inventions there are held by a lot of constraints. From the logical point of view, with regard to ease and tolerance of invention, Hell offered much less difficulty to Milton than Heaven or Earth. *The Christian Doctrine* for instance has hardly anything to say about Satan and Hell since the Bible, on which it is based, says so little about them. That the poem needs, in its teasing out of the Christian truth, to say so much about God and Man, means that Milton's difficulties there are correspondingly greater, and he is provided with fewer degrees of freedom. Here is where we must credit Milton with a great deal of intelligence about the thesis of his poem. A. J. A. Waldock, for example, who is in many ways and about some things in the poem a very sensitive reader, underestimates the amount of thinking that it represents when he writes: 'It is possible, I think, to overrate very much Milton's *awareness* of the peculiar difficulties of his theme. The difficulties are of the kind that fairly leap to our eyes. That is partly because, owing to certain types of literary development during the last two centuries or so, we have received an intensive training in the business of estimating the sort of literary problem that is radical in *Paradise Lost*.'[15] This is to end up with a simpler poem than the one that Milton wrote. Milton knew all about the peculiar difficulties of his theme, and they offered a challenge that makes *Paradise Lost* the lively and intelligent poem that it is.

[15] *Paradise Lost and its Critics* (Cambridge, 1947), p. 17-18.

# 2

# The Presentation of God in Paradise Lost

## I

SINCE the whole intellectual weight of *Paradise Lost* is deliberately exerted towards the thesis that God is provident, we should expect Milton's God and the episodes in which he appears to be developed with some care. Milton looked at God as he was presented in the Bible across a wide area of philosophy and commentary, and he was fully aware of the difficulties with which the believer was faced, and especially of the traditional difficulties of reconciling God's goodness with the existence of evil and God's fore-knowledge with the freedom of Man's will. They were difficulties that could lead to scepticism: that God permitted but was not responsible for evil was a distinction that baffled Hobbes: 'Such distinctions as these dazle my understanding; I finde no difference between the *will* to have a thing done, and the *permission* to do it, when he that permitteth it can hinder it, and knows that it will be done unless he hinder it,'[1] and that God's foreknowledge should nevertheless not determine was one that baffled Hume:

[1] *Of Liberty and Necessity* (1654), p. 23.

The *second* objection admits not of so easy or satisfactory an answer; nor is it possible to explain distinctly how the Deity can be the mediate cause of all the actions of men without being the author of sin and moral turpitude. These are mysteries which mere natural and unassisted reason is very unfit to handle; and whatever system she embraces, she must find herself in inextricable difficulties, and even contradictions at every step which she takes with regard to such subjects. To reconcile the indifference and contingency of human action with prescience, or to defend absolute decrees, and yet free the Deity from being the author of sin, has been found hitherto to exceed all the powers of philosophy. Happy, if she be thence sensible of her temerity, when she pries into these sublime mysteries; and leaving a scene so full of obscurities and perplexities, return with suitable modesty, to her true and proper province, the examination of common life; where she will find difficulties enough to employ her enquiries without launching into so boundless an ocean of doubt, uncertainty and contradiction.[2]

In these two cases the exercise of intelligence makes for scepticism and irony. But Milton's thesis was not sceptical, his intelligence being shown rather in the way that he reads and presents the orthodox case. He is scrupulously concerned to make his narrative illustrate God's proper and necessary attributes.[3] The opening of the poem straightway shows this concern explicitly, in the way in which it describes Hell:

> Such place Eternal Justice had prepar'd
> For these rebellious, here their Prison ordain'd
> In utter darkness . . .
>
> (I, 70-72)

That the devils are in Hell is a manifestation of God's justice, and that God had prepared Hell for them indicates that God's

---

[2] *Enquiry concerning Human Understanding*, Sect. VIII, Part II.

[3] For a reading of *Paradise Lost* which explicates the poem in terms of a hypothesis which is the direct opposite of the one which Milton himself appears to be using, see William Empson, *Milton's God* (London, 1961). I do not think that Empson is right, but it is only because Milton saw the difficulties of his own thesis that Empson's interpretation seems to me possible.

foresight rules out any inadvertency on his part. So, a few
lines later, the description of Satan on the lake

> So stretcht out huge in length the Arch-fiend lay
> Chain'd on the burning Lake, nor ever thence
> Had ris'n or heav'd his head, but that the will
> And high permission of all-ruling Heaven
> Left him at large to his own dark designs,
> That with reiterated crimes he might
> Heap on himself damnation, while he sought
> Evil to others, and enrag'd might see
> How all his malice serv'd but to bring forth
> Infinite goodness, grace and mercy shown
> On man by him seduc't, but on himself
> Treble confusion, wrath and vengeance pour'd.
>
> (I, 209-220)

brings directly into issue the conventional question as to how
God's permitting evil is to be squared with his goodness,
quite explicitly spelling out the right implications of the
episode. But the argument sometimes works less openly and
more subtly. The first episode in Book III, when God and the
Son see Satan emerging from Hell, is very carefully contrived.
Satan's imprisonment and his escape are of course Biblical:

> For if God spared not the angels that sinned, but cast them
> down to hell, and delivered them into chains of darkness, to be
> reserved into judgment . . .
>
> (II Peter 2: 4)

> And cast him into the bottomless pit, and shut him up,
> and set a seal upon him, that he should deceive the nations no
> more . . .
>
> (Revelation 20: 3)

> AND the fifth angel sounded, and I saw a star fall from heaven
> unto the earth: and to him was given the key of the bottomless
> pit.
> 2 And he opened the bottomless pit; and there arose a smoke

out of the pit, as the smoke of a great furnace; and the sun and the air were darkened by reason of the smoke of the pit.

3 And there came out of the smoke locusts upon the earth: and unto them was given power, as the scorpions of the earth have power.

(Revelation 9)

Milton's account of all this is developed very finely. He insists firstly that God sees Satan's escape:

> Onely begotten Son, seest thou what rage
> Transports our adversarie, whom no bounds
> Prescrib'd, no barrs of Hell, nor all the chains
> Heapt on him there, nor yet the main Abyss
> Wide interrupt can hold; so bent he seems
> On desperat reveng, that shall redound
> Upon his own rebellious head.
>
> (III, 80-86)

Milton is right to insist on the fact that God saw Satan (since, being omniscient, he must have seen him) even at the risk of provoking the question as to why since God saw him he did not stop him. For there is a conventional answer to that question: God permits evil and eventually turns it to his own purpose. This is made clear here in God's statement that Satan's evil will redound upon his own head, a divine promise that carries reassurance about God's foreknowledge and goodness. Secondly Milton includes the matter of the bars of Hell, fully measuring the risk. These bars and chains that had been put upon Satan are Biblical. In Book I (210) Satan had been described as 'Chain'd on the burning Lake' and Milton is careful to insist there that Satan moved off the lake only because God permitted him to move (211). So here, it is important that God himself, referring to the apparent failure of the bars of Hell to imprison Satan, goes on to say how Satan will eventually be defeated. The powerful tone in which God asserts his ultimate victory shows that he is not humiliated by Satan's escape, nor inadvertent in failing to provide against it,

24

nor inefficient in having made his bars badly. The reference to the bars is thus ironical, like God's reference in XI, 93 (discussed in the previous chapter) to the possibility that Adam might after the Fall escape the doom of death by eating the fruit of the Tree of Life. Thirdly, by expanding the episode of the actual opening of the pit into Satan's encounter with Sin in Book II, 629-689, Milton gains a useful advantage. Making Sin (who has her own reasons) directly responsible for the opening of the gates of Hell and for Satan's emergence, he is able to avoid seeming to make God directly responsible for it. He is using the distinction (which baffled Hobbes) between God's permitting and God's willing a thing to be done: God did not will Satan's escape but merely permitted Sin to achieve it. The result of all this working is that Milton manages to make God's knowledge and power a very real and important part of the episode in a way that the Biblical passages on which the episode is based do not. God's attributes are thus more fully realized and dramatized in it. Similarly the account of the creation of the world in Book VII, though relying on the Bible for its facts, nevertheless so manipulates those facts that they manifest much more emphatically than they do in Genesis the power and the munificence of God.

II

This realization of God's attributes, and their realization in the right way with the right implications, was a difficult task that Milton had set himself. A good example of the ingenuity that distinguished his treatment can be seen in the way in which the poem presents God's foreknowledge. Clearly this fore-knowledge ruled out some sorts of drama with God, since God does not live in a dimension where suspense is possible. This is why God's speech about the Fall and the Redemption in Book III is made to dispose the events in what is deliberately an unchronological and undramatic order. God promises that Man will find grace (III, 131) before he has apparently found

the volunteer upon whom the provision of grace depends.
God, since he has foreknowledge, knows the answer to his
question

> Which of ye will be mortal to redeem
> Mans mortal crime, and just th'unjust to save,
> Dwels in all Heaven charitie so deare?
>
> (III, 214-216)

before he asks it. Calvin had also characterized as absurd a deity
presented in the way that Milton avoids: 'What could have
been more frigid or absurd than to have represented God as
looking from the height of Heaven to see whence the salvation
of the human race was to come.'[4] That the angels fall silent
when this question is put to them and do nor dare to sacrifice
themselves

> He ask'd, but all the Heav'nly Quire stood mute,
> And silence was in Heav'n: on mans behalf
> Patron or Intercessor none appeerd,
> Much less that durst upon his own head draw
> The deadly forfeiture, and ransom set.
>
> (III, 217-221)

is of course no criticism of their virtue. That there were things
that angels dare not do (without being, because of that, any the
less angelic) is made clear in *The Christian Doctrine* (XV, 105)
where Milton, discussing Jude 1: 9 which says that Michael,
when disputing with the devil about the body of Moses,
durst not bring against him a railing accusation, argues that this
must apply to the angel and not to Christ (with whom Michael
was sometimes identified) since it would be improper to
suggest that Christ dared not do anything. And Christ is, as
Hebrews 1: 4 says, 'made so much better than the angels.' But
the request for a volunteer to suffer death on Man's behalf is
properly put to the angels since they are curious about and
interested in Man's salvation. In *The Christian Doctrine* Milton

---

[4] *Institutes* (Book III, ch. xxii), trans. Beveridge, II, 218.

gets this curiosity on to the right logical line by stating that it
arises out of their love for Man and not out of any insatiable
need (XV, 99) and hence is not the sort of curiosity that would
limit their happiness. It is this curiosity which causes the angels
to feel displeasure and sadness when they hear of Satan's
success with Man, feelings that need to be made (paradoxically)
compatible with their happiness:

> displeas'd
> All were who heard, dim sadness did not spare
> That time Celestial visages, yet mixt
> With pitie, violated not thir bliss.
>
> (X, 22-25)

But Milton's real problem with regard to God's foreknowledge was to differentiate the ways in which it could make for
either despondency or reassurance. The necessitating aspect of
God's providence was of course an important means of reassurance for the faithful. That the just are to be saved and the
unjust punished is after all a source of comfort only on the
supposition that what God says will happen must indeed
happen. Thus God's promise to Adam and Eve that their seed
shall bruise Satan's head is made providentially in order to keep
them from despair, and Adam is shown the future by Michael
in Books XI and XII in order that, being shown what is to
come, his faith may be confirmed. The same reassurance is
provided for the angels in the war in Heaven in a speech of
God's which is often misunderstood. The account of the war is
based on Revelation 12:

> 7 And there was war in Heaven: Michael and his angels fought
> against the dragon; and the dragon fought and his angels,
> 8 And prevailed not; neither was their place found any more in
> Heaven.

The Christian Doctrine makes it clear that Milton interpreted
this to mean that Michael failed to defeat Satan: 'Michael, the
leader of the angels, is introduced in the capacity of a hostile

commander waging war with the prince of the devils, the armies on both sides being drawn out in battle array, and separating after a doubtful conflict' (XV, 105). In the light of this the speech which God makes to the angels before they go to war is very interesting:

> lead forth to Battel these my Sons
> Invincible, lead forth my armed Saints
> By Thousands and by Millions rang'd for fight;
> Equal in number to that Godless crew
> Rebellious, them with Fire and hostile Arms
> Fearless assault, and to the brow of Heav'n
> Pursuing, drive them out from God and bliss . . .
>
> (VI, 46-52)

Although the conflict might be going to be a 'doubtful' one, Milton makes the speech *sound* as little 'doubtful' for the angels as possible. He is anxious not to make it seem that God is grimly tormenting his angels, deliberately setting them a task that he knows they will be unable to perform. Rather, exercising his foreknowledge, God assures their side that they will not be overcome (they are 'Invincible') and that ultimate victory will belong to them, omitting here (what he must foreknow) the role of the Son. Like the Son's own foreknowledge of the triumphant end to his suffering on Earth, 'But I shall rise Victorious, and subdue/My vanquisher' (III, 250-251) the speech is made to communicate power and reassurance. God's foreknowledge thus has for the faithful a welcome providential role.

We can constrast this with the way in which the outcome of another conflict is foretold, this time for Satan.[5] The fight stirring between Gabriel and Satan after the latter's capture by the angelic guard is halted by the sudden appearance of God's golden scales in the sky:

---

[5] See also a discussion of this passage in Sims, *The Bible in Milton's Epics*, pp. 144–146; 178–179.

had not soon
Th'Eternal to prevent such horrid fray
Hung forth in Heav'n his golden Scales, yet seen
Betwixt *Astrea* and the *Scorpion* signe,
Wherein all things created first he weighd,
The pendulous round Earth with ballanc't Aire
In counterpoise, now ponders all events,
Battels and Realms: in these he put two weights
The sequel each of parting and of fight;
The latter quick up flew, and kickt the beam;
Which *Gabriel* spying, thus bespake the Fiend.
    *Satan*, I know thy strength, and thou knowst mine,
Neither our own but giv'n; what follie then
To boast what Arms can doe, since thine no more
Than Heav'n permits, nor mine, though doubld now
To trample thee as mire: for proof look up,
And read thy Lot in yon celestial Sign
Where thou are weigh'd, and shown how light, how weak,
If thou resist. The Fiend lookt up and knew
His mounted Scale aloft: nor more; but fled
Murmuring, and with him fled the shades of night.
                                        (IV, 995-1015)

Milton superbly exploits some apparently risky classical
machinery. There are important differences between his
scales and those of Homer and Virgil. In the first place the
scales in the *Iliad* and the *Aeneid* measure merely outcome: the
lot that sinks is the one that will not prosper (in *Iliad*, VIII, the
Greeks'; XVI, the Trojans'; XXII, Hector's. In *Aeneid*, XII,
Turnus's). But Milton, remembering those Biblical balances in
which Belshazzar was weighed and found wanting (Daniel
5: 27), makes his scales indicate not only outcome but also
value, as Gabriel points out to Satan: 'Where thou are weigh'd
& shown how light, how weak,/If thou resist' (IV, 1012-1013),
an attribute nicely caught by the pun on 'ponders' (not only
*weighs*, but also *meditates on, weighs the value of*). Secondly the
scales in Homer and Virgil are not seen by those whose lots are
being weighed so that they are not a means by which Zeus and

Jupiter communicate their judgments to man. (In *Iliad*, VIII, the Greeks are made aghast not by the scales but by a blazing flash which is sent amongst their army *after* the lots have been weighed; in XVI Hector knows the adverse judgment of the scales when he feels the weakling heart that Zeus has put into him; in XXII, Hector is incited to battle all unaware. In *Aeneid*, XII, Turnus does not see that the fight with Aeneas is going to go against him.) But this either makes the scales a useless device, a poetical fancy, or else implies that Zeus and Jupiter themselves need the scales in order to find out what is going to happen, in which case they are not, as gods, omniscient. Milton's God on the other hand is omniscient and uses the scales not for his own knowledge but to prevent a battle (IV, 996) by giving knowledge to others. Thirdly what God's scales do foretell is interesting. As the future is this time being revealed to Satan, the prophecy does not make for reassurance, although Milton, making a rhetorical identification of God's scales with the Libra constellation which can still be seen, reminds his readers (quite without threat) that God's judgment does not cease. Satan flies 'murmuring,' with Gabriel's contempt sounding in his ears. Furthermore, God's foreknowledge is here interestingly and deliberately made conditional: Satan will be defeated *if* he resists. Milton is making use of a distinction between God's absolute and conditional necessity which he discusses in *The Christian Doctrine* (XIV, 65). It was prompted by those cases in the Bible where things foretold by God, e.g. that Nineveh would be overthrown (Jonah 3: 4), do not come to pass, so that these decrees had to be understood as made conditionally, e.g. that Nineveh would be overthrown *if* it did not repent. This distinction serves nicely here in the poem to illustrate the way in which Satan is both free and not free on Earth. He has God's permission to exercise choice (in this case to flee, later to tempt), but his actions and their outcome are within God's knowledge and God's power, though not, it would appear, determined. By saying what will happen *if* Satan does one thing, Milton's God does not appear to be forcing him to do the other. But the episode leaves us in no doubt as to the inferiority and dependence of Satan. This invention of the scales is one of the intellectual triumphs of the poem.

But God's absolute knowledge could make for despair if it were looked at as something which necessitated. It was important, on the human level, to keep the idea of freedom alive at the same time (the aspect of the matter that baffled Hume). Milton steers his poem very ingeniously on this issue. What happens on Earth has for example necessarily to be dovetailed with what Heaven has already foretold will happen. But whereas this is shown in Heaven as divine foreknowledge, it is not shown on Earth as necessity or destiny. The tactic is not to relate the heavenly and the earthly dimensions to each other in the wrong sort of way. It is proper, for example, when dealing with Satan, for Milton to show that God is continually getting in his way or making him serve God's own purposes.
When in Book X Satan is suddenly and to the utter confounding of his own attempted foreknowledge—'up and enter now into full bliss' (X, 503)—turned into a snake, it is useful to stress that this shows the power of God:

> a greater power
> Now rul'd him, punisht in the shape he sin'd,
> According to his doom . . .
>
> (X, 515-517)

but on Earth it is very necessary to avoid what might seem divine interference. On this level God himself can pretend to the unGod-like feelings of suspense and surprise. Though he knows for example all about the Fall and has foretold it long before, nevertheless in Book X he comes down to the Garden looking for Adam as if trying to find out for himself what has happened. So too in Book VIII, after joking with Adam about the question of Adam's loneliness, God plays out the decision to create Eve on Adam's level, as a kindly answer to Adam's request for company. Only after Adam has shown his wisdom

31

in refusing the company of beasts and solitude does God say
that he foreknew the whole matter:

> I, ere thou spaks't,
> Knew it not good for Man to be alone,
> And no such companie as then thou saw'st,
> Intended thee, for trial onely brought,
> To see how thou could'st judge of fit and meet . . .
> (VIII, 444-448)

To bring in the question of God's foreknowledge last is
to put the business the right way round. It shows how well
God understands and supplies Man's nature whereas to bring it
in first would reduce Man to a puppet.

The fact that the earthly dimension can be presented in
greater detail also serves to appear to give it some independence
of the heavenly foreknowledge. The most telling example of
earthly complication fitting in with heavenly simplicity is the
Fall itself. In Book IX all is done out of human decision, and the
Fall unfolds in a series of human problems. God has already
foretold it, but his foreknowledge is here kept apart from the
foretold event and is fulfilled (as it is not in the case of Satan's
becoming the serpent) without comment. Adam and Eve in
Book IX never cease to look like free and responsible agents of
their own affairs. So too after the Fall, with his decision in
Book X to have children and perpetuate human life, Adam by
free will and resolution comes to a decision which God has
already known, since his judgment on them earlier refers to
their seed (X, 180):

> Then let us seek
> Some safer resolution, which methinks
> I have in view, calling to minde with heed
> Part of our Sentence, that thy Seed shall bruise
> The Serpents head; piteous amends, unless
> Be meant, whom I conjecture, our grand Foe
> *Satan*, who in the Serpent hath contriv'd
> Against us this deceit: to crush his head

> Would be revenge indeed; which will be lost
> By death brought on our selves, or childless days
> Resolv'd, as thou proposest; so our Foe
> Shall scape his punishment ordain'd, and wee
> Instead shall double ours upon our heads.
>
> (X, 1028-1040)

Adam can as a matter of fact no more escape not committing suicide than Satan can escape being turned into a snake, but Milton does not, in Adam's case, stress that aspect of the matter. Here Adam's sudden realization of the fact that God has foreknown their seed, turns that foreknowledge into a reassurance. What is a doom for Satan is a promise for Adam, and God's providence is thus seen as reasonable and good and aiming at the relief of human distress. The philosophical problem of reconciling God's foreknowledge and human freedom is thus made less difficult by the way in which the poem is organized, and the disposition of the narrative is very much part of the argument. That the proper handling of an episode can thus encourage the believer to think rightly can be seen in the way in which *The Pilgrim's Progress* handles the same problem. Before Christian and Faithful come to Vanity Fair, they are confronted by Evangelist who tells them what will happen to them when they reach that city—that they will be beset with enemies and persecuted, that one of them will be killed (he does not say which), but that 'be you faithful unto death, and the King will give you a Crown of life.'[6] Using his foreknowledge, Evangelist, like Milton's God, is prophetic and exhortative. But while he communicates security, he does not encourage complacency, nor does he let his foreknowledge make a mockery of the free virtue of his hearers. Though he must know also that one of them *will* be faithful unto death, his phrase 'but be ye faithful unto death,' being conditional, saves their liberty of choice.

---

[6] Ed. Wharey (Oxford, 1960), p. 87.

III

Milton moves equally carefully with the presentation of God's attributes of anger and pity. The logical demands of the case need here to be especially looked to if the representation is to be rightly understood. God's anger was a fact of his nature, and it was an anger that was necessarily just and reasonable. If God created Hell it was because his severity could justly send sinners to it. Dramatizing that anger in Book III, Milton was committed to dramatizing an anger that was simple and pure, utterly free of reluctance and pity. God must mean and perform what he says. If he were without reason to remit the threatened punishment for sin, then he might remit a pardon without reason too. God cannot be sympathetic to those against whom his wrath is directed: 'All sinnes are debts; all God's debts must be discharged. It is a bold word but a true; God should not be just, if any of his debts should pass unsatisfied. The conceit of the profane vulgar makes him a God of all mercies, and therefore hopes for pardon without payment.'[7] God's anger was both an historical and a logical fact. Herbert's poem 'Love,' proceeding also like *Paradise Lost* through the full cycle of God's relationship with Man, includes the same attributes:

> Love bade me welcome: yet my soul drew back
>     Guiltie of dust and sinne.
> But quick-ey'd Love, observing me grow slack
>     From my first entrance in,
> Drew nearer to me, sweetly questioning,
>     If I lack'd anything.
>
> A guest, I answer'd, worthy to be here:
>     Love said, You shall be he.
> I the unkinde, ungratefull? Ah my deare,
>     I cannot look on thee.
> Love took my hand, and smiling did reply,
>     Who made the eyes but I?

[7] Joseph Hall, *Heaven Upon Earth.* (*Works* (1625), p. 77.)

Truth Lord, but I have marr'd them: let my shame
Go where it doth deserve.
And know you not, sayes Love, who bore the blame?
My deare, then I will serve.
You must sit down, sayes Love, and taste my meat:
So I did sit and eat.

Man's humiliation before God is here answered by the history
of God's dealings with Man. Herbert moves from the Creation
('Who made the eyes but I?'), to the Fall ('Truth Lord, but I
have marr'd them') and the consequent and just condemnation
of Man ('Let my shame/Go where it doth deserve'), finally to
the Atonement ('And know you not, sayes Love, who bore the
blame?'). The process involves the same God as Milton's,
and the same words ('blame' and 'ungrateful') are used. The
only difference is that in Herbert 'blame' is used by the one who
by his death restored Man to bliss, and not by the one who,
angry at the offence, justly imposed the penalty; and 'ungrateful' is used by the offender, Man, and not, as it is in
Milton—'Ingrate, he had of mee' (III, 97)—by the one who was
offended. But the logic of the two cases is the same: Herbert's
Love is, as Herbert shows, creator, judge and redeemer.

And God's anger, if it is just, must be unmixed with pity.
To ascribe pity to God in such a case would, since God has
created Man's world and Man's nature, indict that providence
which *Paradise Lost* is written to assert. Milton is very insistent
on this need to regard without pity those episodes representing
God's anger and justice. One of Raphael's difficulties in
recounting the fall of the angels to Adam is the necessity for the
story to be told and listened to without pity:

High matter, thou injoinst me, O prime of men,
Sad task and hard, for how shall I relate
To human sense th'invisible exploits
Of warring Spirits; how without remorse
The ruin of so many glorious once
And perfet while they stood . . .
(V, 563-568)

35

Raphael has the problem which Milton himself has of ensuring that his work implies the right things and arouses the correct response. Similarly God, instructing Michael to banish Adam and Eve from the garden after the Fall, tells him to do this without pity:

> Hast thee, and from the Paradise of God
> Without remorse drive out the sinful Pair . . .
> (XI, 104-105)

Pity would be improper in this situation where God is bent upon punishment and rebuke: what has befallen Adam and Eve is just and of their own responsibility. The danger that pity involves can be seen in this speech of Satan's on his first sight of Adam and Eve:

> Ah gentle pair, yee little think how nigh
> Your change approaches, when all these delights
> Will vanish and deliver ye to woe,
> More woe, the more your tast is now of joy;
> Happie, but for so happie ill secur'd
> Long to continue, and this high seat your Heav'n
> Ill fenc't for Heav'n to keep out such a foe
> As now is enter'd . . .
> (IV, 366-373)

The speech's 'charm' disguises its erroneous implications. Satan's pity is one that indicts God's providence: it would be one thing to pity Adam and Eve after the Fall as his victims, but it is something else to say as he does that Adam and Eve are badly adapted to their situation. Satan's pity is for their frailty and exposedness, but this is to blame God who made them what they are.

Pity has necessarily to be ruled out where God's justice is concerned. The certainty of his vengeance and the justness of its operation guarantee the equal certainty of his love and justness if he is obeyed. It is Milton's concern for this justice that prompts his introduction before the Fall of the idea (V, 493) that if Adam and Eve remain obedient to God's will then their bodies will in course of time turn to spirit and they will become like angels, inhabitants of Heaven. Milton is worried about the idea of the Fortunate Fall. It is one thing to say that Adam is, as a result of the Atonement, better off than he was in Paradise, but something altogether different to suggest that he is better off than he would have been if he had stayed obedient. God's mercy cannot be allowed to make nonsense of his justice. That is why God, once Man has disobeyed, has to insist on his justice being fully satisfied by the forfeit of a life before he can make Man the object of his mercy and grace. The operation of his mercy in his forgiveness of Man was not arbitrary. It had, too, important warrant in the fact that Man fell not wholly of his own accord but tempted by Satan.[8] That is how God himself justifies his mercy when it is ordained:

> The first sort by thir own suggestion fell,
> Self-tempted, self-deprav'd: Man falls deceiv'd
> By th'other first: Man therefore shall find grace,
> The other none . . .
>
> (III, 129-132)

It is this that justifies the pity which the angels feel (X, 25) when they hear of the fall of Man: though 'displeas'd' (X, 22) at Man's disobedience, they can still also pity him, not as the subject of God's justice but as the victim of Satan. Although Man was providentially given his defences against temptation, nevertheless Satan's role provided some excuse for Man that could not apply to the case of the fallen angels or of Satan himself. It is his awareness of the importance of Satan in the fall of Man that made Milton go so carefully in his account of the fall of the angels. At first sight it might appear as though there is a certain cursoriness and weakness in some aspects of Milton's treatment (and especially in the inadequacy of some of Satan's speeches).[9] But Milton's hands are tied. Although Satan

[8] John S. Diekhoff, *Milton's Paradise Lost: A Commentary on the Argument* (New York and London, 1946), pp. 98-104, has a good discussion of the whole issue. My own treatment is more concerned with the contradiction in the narrative.

[9] See John Peter, *A Critique of Paradise Lost* (New York and London, 1960), pp. 68-72.

is 'the Author of all ill' (II, 381) and therefore has to lead in subtlety, Milton cannot show him as winning over the other angels in very clever speeches. If the fallen angels had been so persuaded by Satan, then it would have been unjust of God not to arrange some mercy for them as he was later to do for Man. So Satan's first speech with Beelzebub, though it does what Satan's nominal role as leader in ill requires,

> So spake the false Arch-Angel, and infus'd
> Bad influence into th'unwarie brest
> Of his Associate . . .
>
> (V, 694-696)

nevertheless is still not responsible for Beelzebub's fall. As a speech it is still no more than an order to get the other angels to assemble. Similarly, when Satan does address the other angels (V, 772-802), Milton rightly treats the occasion as a public debate, not as a temptation. This helps to make the decision all the more an individual one for each angel to make. This is where Abdiel's role is crucial and why he was invented. The fact that *he* is shown to have made his own decision (V, 809-848) means that all the other angels must have made their own too. Their fall is thus wholly of their own will. The sleight of hand that Milton is adopting is obvious enough, but all the inadequacies of the narrative can here be laid wholly at the door of the (contradictory) logic of the theme. Milton is organizing the matter in order this time to justify God's providence in its *lack* of mercy.

But God's pity has another important aspect: it is never merely feeling but is necessarily active. Thus when God sees Adam and Eve in the Garden and sends Raphael to warn them of the danger that they are in from Satan, Milton makes a nice point about God's pity:

> Them thus imploid beheld
> With pittie Heav'ns high King, and to him call'd
> *Raphael*, the sociable Spirit, that deign'd

38

To travel with *Tobias*, and secur'd
His marriage with the seaventimes-wedded Maid.
(V. 219-223)

God's pity here is justified by the traditional distinction between God's permitting a thing to be done and his willing it to be done. Although God permitted Satan to enter the Garden and did not propose to hinder him in his design to tempt Man, God did not ordain the Fall. It is the presence of Satan in this scene that makes God's pity possible. And that pity is an active thing, more than mere feeling or words, since it leads immediately to the despatch of Raphael in order to exhort and warn Man. Similarly, God's pity in Book X is active and leads God to clothe his creatures:

> then pittying how they stood
> Before him naked to the aire, that now
> Must suffer change, disdain'd not to begin
> Thenceforth the form of servant to assume,
> As when he wash'd his servants feet so now
> As Father of his Familie he clad
> Thir nakedness with Skins of Beasts . . .
> (X, 211-217)

The justification here is also elaborate. The episode is in Genesis and hence must be consistent with God's justice. Its propriety in the poem is established by the Son himself who makes it clear that the action is not arbitrary or inconsistent but firmly founded on right and law:

> I go to judge
> On Earth these thy transgressors, but thou knowst,
> Whoever judg'd, the worst on mee must light,
> When time shall be, for so I undertook
> Before thee; and, not repenting, this obtaine
> Of right, that I may mitigate thir doom
> On me deriv'd, yet I shall temper so
> Justice with Mercie, as may illustrate most
> Them fully satisfied, and thee appease.
> (X, 71-79)

D

39

This is apologetic, laying down theoretical justification (which Genesis lacks) for the clothing episode which Genesis committed Milton to. Once this justification is established, then, although God's justice ordained death as a punishment for disobedience, his mercy can still cover Man's nakedness and ultimately transform the punishment into a providential remedy and solace: 'so Death becomes/His final remedie' (XI, 61-62).

This active role of God is also reflected in his speeches in the poem which are always purposive, initiating action. The speeches of Book III (80-343) announce the judgment and also the provision of redemption for fallen Man; those in Book V lead to the despatch of Raphael to warn Adam and Eve of their danger (224-245) and to the exaltation of the Son (600-615); those in Book VI initiate various moves in the war in Heaven; those of Book VII ordain the creation of the world; God's conversation with Adam in Book VIII prefaces his creation of Eve; the first speech in Book X despatches the Son as redeemer and friend as well as judge (34-62), the second imposes the curse of Death upon the world in order to cleanse it of its stain of sin (616-640); the speech of Book XI despatches Michael to expel Adam and Eve from the Garden but also to comfort them about their future (99-125). This *active* and providential concern is a most important and necessary attribute of God's nature.

Thus Milton's God is a figure drawn absolutely in accord with the logic of the case. It is carried through with a great deal of forethought and hard thinking, prompted by the need to look very intently at the implications of any particular scene. *The Christian Doctrine* does precisely that in its teasing out of what the various texts in the Bible say or imply about the nature of God, and *Paradise Lost* is in no way a betrayal of that sort of careful, logical thinking.

# 3

# The Garden

## I

THE presentation of life on Earth is developed equally systematically, and its beauty is logical as well as poetic. Addison, travelling in France, came across a French capucin who 'laid it down as Point of Doctrine, that Laughter was the Effect of Original Sin, and that *Adam* could not laugh before the Fall.'[1] Milton would have understood this sort of casuistical thinking about what life was like before the Fall, though he would not have agreed with the capucin's doctrine since there is mirth in his Garden. His scenes celebrate the good and innocent life and owe much to classical precedent and contemporary taste, but since they need to be made consistent with what Genesis says and with the poem's hypothesis about the rationality and goodness of God, there is a strong logical element in Milton's picture.[2] This was welcome since Milton's

[1] *Spectator*, No. 249.

[2] For useful and interesting discussions of these scenes see: Williams, *The Common Expositor*, pp. 66-111 (an account of the problems and interpretations of the commentators on Genesis); Sister Irma Corcoran, *Milton's Paradise with Reference to the Hexameral Background* (Washington, D.C., 1945); Arnold Stein, *Answerable Style* (Minneapolis, 1953), pp. 52-74; Isabel MacCaffrey, *Paradise Lost as 'Myth'* (Cambridge, Mass., 1959), pp. 148-156 (these last two concerned with the style and images of the scenes); J. B. Broadbent, *Some Graver Subject* (London, 1960), pp. 169-201 (including details of the traditional elements in the picture); Frank Kermode, 'Adam Unparadised,' *The Living Milton*, ed. Kermode (London, 1960), pp. 107-116 (on the Garden of love).

pastoral thus offered the opportunity for invention as well as for imitation. One of the difficulties of pastoral, as Johnson saw, was that it provided too few occasions for originality: the pleasures of the country were, on his view, real enough but unchanging.[3] The poets had done their best to bring new life to the theme of idyllic bliss. There was the possibility of a change of occupation, from shepherd to gardener (as in *Paradise Lost*) or to mower (as in Theocritus' *Tenth Idyll* and in Marvell), or even (with piscatory eclogues or *The Compleat Angler*) to fishermen. Marvell's 'The Garden' shows, for example, what can be done with the pastoral of wit, and although Milton's pastoral has necessarily to be more serious, Milton too knows the sort of game that can be played. Marvell, fully aware of the erotic conventions of pastoral, makes his pastoral a celibate's paradise; Milton, equally unusually, makes the life in his Garden marital and domestic. Marvell's garden is a paradise of leisure and idleness; Milton's provides labour of a uniquely light kind.

Milton's Garden is based necessarily on Genesis, and his pastoral is thus committed to a logical extension and sometimes to a logical straightening out of what Genesis says. He provides, for example, more elaborate accounts of Adam and Eve's diet, and because he is describing a radically innocent way of life ordained by a provident Creator, he is forced to proceed deductively. The drink which Adam and Eve press from the grape is an 'inoffensive moust' (V, 345) because drunkenness cannot exist before the Fall, a fact that comes usefully to hand in similes describing the effect of the forbidden Fruit upon Adam and Eve when they become 'hight'nd as with Wine, jocond and boon' (IX, 793) and 'As with new Wine intoxicated both' (IX, 1008). Similarly, the shrub with which Eve scents the ground has to be 'unfum'd (V, 349) since Man does not before the Fall have the use of fire. It is because of this that Milton, with some humour, says of their meal 'No fear lest Dinner coole' (V, 396). The line represents some sophistication. Adam

[3] *Rambler*, No. 36.

and Eve may not be able to have hot meals, but this sounds not improvident when the disadvantages of hot meals are considered, viz. that they sometimes get cold. The manner in which the Garden is watered also provides a nice point. Genesis 2: 5-6 says that the earth is without rain though there is a mysterious dewfall, but it appears later in the same chapter (v. 10) that there is a river which waters the Garden. Genesis does not say how this river is replenished, nor whether there is thereafter rain. Milton's Garden however is typically unmagical and is watered by mists and showers. Since there are no storms to disturb Eden—there were storms at sea but they come under a different system, showing the power of God— Milton is careful always to stress the gentleness and fragrance of the showers in Paradise (see IV, 653; V, 190). So when he provides a storm to mark the moment of Man's fall,

> Skie lowr'd, and muttering Thunder, som sad drops
> Wept at compleating of the mortal Sin . . .
> (IX, 1002-1003)

he is not merely improving an occasion as Shakespeare is with the storm in *Lear*. He is describing what logically had to be the first thunder shower. The conventional conceit of tears as rain is brought within the same pattern; the tears of the unfallen Eve are gentle like the showers of the Garden before the Fall:

> But silently a gentle tear let fall
> From either eye, and wip't them with her haire;
> Two other precious drops that ready stood,
> Each in thir Chrystal sluce, hee ere they fell
> Kiss'd as the gracious signs of sweet remorse . . .
> (V, 130-134)

whereas tears after the Fall are wild, like storms:

> They sate them down to weep, nor onely Teares
> Raind at thir Eyes, but high Winds worse within . . .
> (IX, 1121-1122)

Milton had of course to look especially carefully at God's

command to tend the Garden (Genesis 2: 15). The work
cannot be onerous since labour is one of the things that God
ordains for Man as a consequence of the Fall (Genesis 3: 19). So,
Adam and Eve are provided with tools whose origin, since
there is no fire, needs explanation: 'such Gardning Tools as
Art yet rude,/ Guiltless of fire had formd, or Angels brought'
(IX, 391-392). Paradox also comes to the aid of this concept of
unlaborious work:

> They sat them down, and after no more toil
> Of thir sweet Gardning labour then suffic'd
> To recommend coole *Zephyr*, and made ease
> More easie . . .
>
> (IV, 327-330)

God's goodness is here also exemplified in his provision of
remedy, a cooling breeze by day (and sleep by night). Indeed
Milton makes the command to work itself a mark of God's
providence. None of the other creatures are so exhorted, so
that the command can be read as a mark of Man's uniqueness,
as Milton's Adam—though not the Adam of Genesis—points
out:

> other Creatures all day long
> Rove idle unimploid, and less need rest;
> Man hath his daily work of body or mind
> Appointed, which declares his Dignitie.
>
> (IV, 616-619)

But the word in Genesis that causes Milton most difficulty is
'subdue': '28 And God blessed them, and God said unto them,
Be fruitful and multiply, and replenish the earth, and subdue
it' (Genesis I). Since the word might seem to suggest some
wildness on the Garden's part, some possible misrule, Milton
has to make it clear that this represents no threat to Man.
His first tactic is to read the Garden's wildness as an aspect of its
enormous fertility, and hence as an exemplification of the
profusion of God's goodness. The common enough distinction
between art and nature, between control and abundance,

helped to carry him across this problem of the Garden that, though innocent, needed to be subdued:

> Flours worthy of Paradise which not nice Art
> In Beds and curious Knots, but Nature boon
> Powrd forth profuse on Hill and Dale and Plaine . . .
>
> (IV, 241-243)

His second tactic is to link the wildness of the Garden with God's command to the human pair to multiply (Genesis 1: 28) so that God's promise of children is remedial, providing assistance for their work:

> These paths & Bowers doubt not but our joynt hands
> Will keep from Wilderness with ease, as wide
> As we need walk, till younger hands ere long
> Assist us . . .
>
> (IX, 244-247)

Here again the typical systematization is at work, stitching up the various exhortations in Genesis about life in the Garden into a more coherent pattern than Genesis itself provides.

## II

A most important aspect of Milton's Paradise is the sort and variety of relationship that it offers. Genesis clearly indicates that this was something that God was anxious to furnish since Eve was created as a remedy against Adam's loneliness (Genesis 2: 18). Milton's God provides even more extensively against it. The virtue of friendship was important to Milton in his own life, and Adam and Eve are not left deficient in that intellectual companionship which is an integral part of the good life. They have friends of the highest possible sort, as the opening of Book IX shows:

> No more of talk where God or Angel Guest
> With Man, as with his Friend, familiar us'd
> To sit indulgent, and with him partake
> Rural repast . . .
>
> (IX, 1-4)

45

But it is the relationship between Adam and Eve that is naturally developed most fully in the poem. Milton's ideas about marriage and divorce were anyway deductions from Biblical material so that this sort of thinking about Genesis was a familiar enough process to him. Milton was obviously committed to a naked and unashamed Adam and Eve in the Garden before the Fall since that is what Genesis says: '25 And they were both naked, the man and his wife, and were not ashamed' (Genesis 2), and Man's degradation after the Fall was clearly marked by the onset of sexual shame, since Adam, being naked, hid himself (Genesis 3: 10). Genesis did not commit a writer to unfallen sexuality as necessarily as it committed him to unfallen nakedness, but Milton adopts the thesis that there was an unfallen, innocent sexuality. It can naturally be seen as part of God's instituting of marriage for Adam and Eve in his injunction to them to multiply. And it was something in which Milton anyway believed.

His thesis in the poem about it has some interesting and ingenious features. He still insists on associating sex with privacy. This concept of the privacy of unfallen love arises not at all out of any uneasinesses on Milton's part but quite simply out of his view of marriage as the institution of a special and private relationship, one meant for Man and not for the beasts. There is clearly a special oneness between husband and wife since, as Genesis says, a man will leave his father and mother and cleave to his wife (Genesis, 2: 24). So, even before the Fall, the sexual parts are 'mysterious' (IV, 312), so are the rites of love (IV, 742), and wedded love has, in the Garden, an unusual exclusiveness and sense of particular belonging:

> Haile wedded Love, mysterious Law, true source
> Of human ofspring, sole proprietie,
> In Paradise of all things common else.
>
> (IV, 750-752)

Thus shame and modesty, of a pure unfallen sort, are a natural part of prelapsarian love. Eve blushes when Adam leads her to

46

the nuptial bower (VIII, 511), and the mention of angelic sexuality also makes Raphael blush:

> To whom the Angel with a smile that glow'd
> Celestial rosie red, Loves proper hue,
> Answer'd.
>
> (VIII, 618-620)

The blush is 'proper' because it springs out of that 'proprietie' of relationship which belongs to true love. Although C. S. Lewis found some of the suggestions in the descriptions of Eve offensive and inappropriate,[4]

> Shee as a vail down to the slender waste
> Her unadorned golden tresses wore
> Dissheveld, but in wanton ringlets wav'd
> As the Vine curles her tendrils, which impli'd
> Subjection, but requir'd with gentle sway,
> And by her yeilded, by him best receivd,
> Yielded with coy submission, modest pride,
> And sweet reluctant amorous delay.
>
> (IV, 304-311)

they must be seen as presented intentionally and not carelessly or inconsistently. Milton's awareness of the difficulties that arise out of his insistence on privacy, female submissiveness and an unfallen sort of shame shows in his recourse to paradox. Eve's tresses are 'wanton' but nevertheless imply 'subjection'; her 'sway' is 'gentle'; her coyness is not baffling or thwarting (as in Marvell's 'To his Coy Mistress') but instead is submissive; her 'pride' is 'modest'; her reluctance not galling but 'sweet'; her 'delay' not denying but 'amorous.' All this manner of description exploits the puzzles in the matter. The same tactic of oxymoron is used in Adam's description of Eve's yielding to him, when he refers to her 'obsequious Majestie' (VIII, 509). There was clearly some logical fun and wit to be won from the business.

---

[4] *Preface to Paradise Lost* (Oxford, 1942), p. 118.

It is Milton's sense of the necessary privacy of unfallen love that leads to his invention of the nuptial bower for Adam and Eve. Milton knew very well the sort of the thing that went on in bowers and sheds and private places in the fallen world as his sarcastic account of More in the *Second Defence* shows:

He happened to be seized with a lawless passion for a servant girl of his host; and though the girl was married not long after to another, he still followed her; the neighbours had frequently observed them enter together a small lodge in the little garden. This amounts not, it may be said, to adultery; he might have been employed about something else. True, he might have been talking with her, for example, on the subject of gardening; he might have taken occasion from gardens, from those of Alcinous, suppose, or of Adonis, to introduce certain lecturings of his to the woman, who might have been a prodigy of understanding, and eager to listen. He might now have praised the parterres; might even have wished for nothing more than shade; might have been allowed no other liberty than to engraft a mulberry in a fig, thence to raise, with the utmost dispatch, a line of sycamores—a most delectable walk. Then he might have taught the woman the art of engrafting.

(VIII, 31-33)

If bowers and gardens offer convenient privacy for illicit love, it would have been unjust of God not to provide a private bower for Adam and Eve's wedded love. The bower reveals God's providence in another respect, in that its function is also to provide shade. The paradisal sun is directly overhead at noon when the Garden receives the full effect of its fructifying power. Milton might have decided to see Adam and Eve as indifferent to heat, in which case there would have to be a change in their natures after the Fall when, as Book X (653) shows, they suffer from heat and cold. But Genesis makes it sound as though God himself enjoyed a wholesome coolness since it was in the 'cool of the day' (Genesis, 3: 8) that he walked in the Garden. So God, 'the sovran Planter' (IV, 691), has provided the bower as a remedy against heat and for the pleasures of shade, and when Raphael visits Adam he finds him making proper use of it:

> Him through the spicie Forrest onward com
> *Adam* discernd, as in the dore he sat
> Of his coole Bowre, while now the mounted Sun
> Shot down direct his fervid Raies, to warme
> Earths inmost womb, more warmth then *Adam* needs.
>
> (V, 298-302)

Adam's being there at noon marks of course an important and characteristic systematization of their lives. Milton has imposed a regimen that is lacking in Genesis. Adam and Eve wake at dawn, there is a natural dinner hour (noon) and supper time. After dinner there is a siesta. The various details of their lives are thus at all points smoothed out into order and pattern, a reflection of the divine reason which has provided this sort of life for them.

### III

The beasts of Paradise[5] are also made to fit the system. God in Genesis gave Adam dominion over all the creatures but Milton did not take this to imply that the animals needed to be tamed. In the Garden they are naturally well-behaved:

> About them frisking playd
> All Beasts of th'Earth, since wilde, and of all chase
> In Wood or Wilderness, Forrest or Den;
> Sporting the Lion rampd, and in his paw
> Dandl'd the Kid; Bears, Tygers, Ounces, Pards,
> Gambold before them, th'unwieldy Elephant
> To make them mirth us'd all his might, and wreathd
> His Lithe Proboscis . . .
>
> (IV, 340-347)

and this friendliness of their manner enables Milton to make a nice point about the difference between the unfallen and the

[5] On these, see Kester Svendsen, *Milton and Science* (Cambridge, Mass., 1956), pp. 137-173.

fallen satanic world, for when Satan a few lines later takes upon himself the shapes of various animals in order to spy upon Adam and Eve, he becomes the animals as they are in their savage post-lapsarian state:

> about them round
> A Lion now he stalkes with fierie glare,
> Then as a Tyger, who by chance hath spi'd
> In some Purlieu two gentle Fawnes at play,
> Strait couches close, then rising changes oft
> His couchant watch, as one who chose his ground
> Whence rushing he might surest seize them both
> Grip't in each paw . . .
>
> (IV, 401-408)

This is a logical point to make and it suits the poem's mode of thought, so that Johnson is quite right to cavil when the logic breaks down as it does in Raphael's comparison of the fleeing demons to a timorous flock (VI, 857): 'The angel, in a comparison, speaks of "timorous deer" before deer were yet timorous, and before Adam could understand the comparison.'[6] But Johnson picks out the one error and ignores all the successes.

These beasts who were Adam's familiars were the land animals. Adam had of course been given power also over the fishes and creatures of the sea but his existence was a land-locked one. The sea was different. The Bible gave ample warrant for Milton to suppose that if God's munificence and loving care were shown in the Garden, then his terrible might was shown in the sea, the 'monstrous world' (Lycidas, 158). God's power was for instance manifest in the leviathan (see Job 41) whose hugeness offers an appropriate image for Satan in Book I, 200-208. God's making of these creatures of the deep is impressively described in Book VII:

> And God created the great Whales . . .
> . . . part huge of bulk

---

[6] Lives of the Poets, ed. Birkbeck Hill, I, 187.

Wallowing unwieldie, enormous in thir Gate
Tempest the Ocean: there Leviathan
Hugest of living Creatures, on the Deep
Stretcht like a Promontorie sleeps or swimmes,
And seems a moving Land, and at his Gilles
Draws in, and at his Trunck spouts out a Sea.

(VII, 391 . . . 410-416)

In this element the vastness and unwieldiness of leviathan are no indictment of God's providence. They are not accidental or inadvertent, evidence of bad design, since they are made purposefully. Creating tempest, they demonstrate the overwhelming might of God. And they do not harm Adam in any way because their life is entirely separate from his. But with this distinction between the land and sea animals in mind, it is easy to see why Milton made his elephant in Paradise a comic turn. What is significant about the elephant is his size and bulkiness:

scarse from his mould
*Behemoth* biggest born of Earth upheav'd
His vastness . . .

(VII, 470-472)

and in the Garden he is called 'unwieldy' (IV, 345). This unwieldiness would do very well for a beast of the sea, but Milton, thinking hard about final causes in respect of a provident God, has to create a purpose for that unwieldiness in the Garden. He ascribes to it a comic role. The elephant's oddity becomes a circus act designed providentially to please the human pair, 'to make them mirth' (IV, 346).

The manner in which *Paradise Lost* presents the serpent is also conditioned by the logic of the case.[7] Before the Fall it is not harmful. This seems a logical enough point to make, but not all accounts of the Fall story had made it. Other writers go wrong precisely because they do not pay enough

---

[7] On the serpent, see Svendsen, *Milton and Science*, pp. 165-170. McCaffrey, *Paradise Lost as 'Myth,'* p. 168 notes the association of the sea-dragon with darkness and sin. My point is with the distinction between the two types of serpent.

attention to the full logical thinking through of their material.[8] Du Bartas, for instance, comments on Satan's decision to use the snake as an instrument for deceit as follows:

> remembring that of all the broods
> In Mountains, Plains, Airs, waters, wilds and woods
> The knotty Serpent's spotty generation
> Are filled with infections inflamation.[9]

He goes on to say that before the Fall the snake does move upright and does not arouse horror, but he fails to explain its prelapsarian venomousness. The *Adamus Exul* has snakes that creep and whose dark poison the cautious are warned to avoid.[10] The *Adamo Caduto* ascribes to the unfallen Eve an altogether feminine horror of vipers and snakes but does not see the need to make this logically plausible.[11] Milton on the other hand is much more alert and his serpent is a very refined and complicated affair. Its poison is, sensibly, a function of Man's corruption:

> Of huge extent sometimes, with brazen Eyes
> And hairie Main terrific, though to thee
> Not noxious, but obedient at thy call.
>
> (VII, 496-498)

This description of Raphael's stresses not merely the serpent's harmlessness but also its obedience to Adam, the latter arising naturally out of God's granting to Adam the dominion over all creatures. But Raphael is also clearly making a discrimination about snakes. Some arouse terror ('sometimes ... terrific'), but others arouse wonder and delight:

> some of Serpent kinde
> Wondrous in length and corpulence involv'd
> Thir Snakie foulds, and added wings.
>
> (VII, 482-484)

[8] Watson Kirkconnell, *The Celestial Cycle* (Toronto, 1952) provides a most useful collection of works, extracts and translations on the subject of the Fall.
[9] Sylvester, *Second Weeke*, Pt. II, ll. 124-127 (*Works*, ed. G. B. Grosart, Chertsey Worthies' Library (1880), I, 108).
[10] Act II, 1.625. See Kirkconnell, p. 135.
[11] Act I, sc. III. See Kirkconnell, p. 294.

It was of course this second sort of serpent that tempted Eve:

> pleasing was his shape,
> And lovely, never since of Serpent kind
> Lovelier . . .
>
> (IX, 503-505)

The distinction is between the land serpent and the sea serpent, the latter being the dragon which Satan was eventually to be associated with: 'And I stood upon the sand of the sea, and saw a beast arise up out of the sea, having seven heads and ten horns, and upon his horns ten crowns, and upon his heads the name of blasphemy' (Revelation 13: 1). Hence also the reference to Pharaoh as the 'River-dragon' (XII, 191) which, being in the sea, could, like leviathan, safely and not improvidentially be allowed an awesome role. The land serpent on the other hand is harmless, obedient and an object of wonder. Genesis also committed Milton to making it subtle '(Now the serpent was more subtil than any beast of the field' (Genesis 3: 1)), and, since the snake was inarticulate, Milton found its motion a useful way of dramatizing that subtlety:

> close the Serpent sly
> Insinuating, wove with Gordian twine
> His breaded train, and of his fatal guile
> Gave proof unheeded . . .
>
> (IV, 347-350)

Milton is quite aware of the danger he is running of making God seem improvident in thus creating slyness in one of his creatures. He saves his thesis by making that slyness quite visible and apparent (even if, through Man's fault, it went unheeded). Nor was that sly motion itself easy to realize. Since the serpent was cursed after the Fall by being made to go upon its belly (Genesis 3: 14), it follows that it must before that have gone upright. But it cannot have gone fully upright since full uprightness was unique to Man:

a Creature who not prone
And Brute as other Creatures, but endu'd
With Sanctitie of Reason, might erect
His Stature, and upright with Front serene
Govern the rest . . .

(VII, 506-510)

Thus, before the Fall, the serpent is a creeping thing that goes upright, and Milton's lines about its involved mode of progress are an attempt to reconcile these two characteristics:

not with indented wave,
Prone on the ground, as since, but on his reare,
Circular base of rising foulds, that tour'd
Fould above fould, a surging Maze, his Head
Crested aloft, and Carbuncle his Eyes;
With burnisht Neck of verdant Gold, erect
Amidst his circling Spires, that on the grass
Floted redundant . . .

(IX, 496-503)

The case gets even more complicated after the Fall. Since God's curse was necessarily fulfilled, the serpent then goes no longer upright, but prone. Clearly, as the commentators saw, the curse was meant mysteriously and aimed not at the snake but at Satan within the snake. In so far as the snake itself was cursed (for the snake now does go upon its belly), Milton has to insist upon the justice of that, since Genesis cannot include an injustice. In his usual dogged way Milton does not suppress the difficulty, but his attempt to square the matter with God's providence sounds little more than bluff:

Which when the Lord God heard, without delay
To Judgement he proceeded on th'accus'd
Serpent though brute, unable to transferre
The Guilt on him who made him instrument
Of mischief, and polluted from the end
Of his creation; justly then accurst

As vitiated in Nature: more to know
Concern'd not Man (since he no further knew)
Nor alter'd his offence; yet God at last
To Satan first in sin his doom apply'd
Though in mysterious terms, judg'd as then best:
And on the Serpent thus his curse let fall.

(X, 163-174)

The phrase 'though brute' points to Milton's uneasiness. The serpent had no responsibility for its being used by Satan, but since it does still go upon its belly it was clearly unable to shift the curse, and the point that it was vitiated in nature is made in order to square the facts somehow with reason. Genesis of course displays no concern whatever about the justice of the curse on the serpent since it does not say that the serpent was taken over by Satan. But the important thing is that the curse was really aimed mysteriously at Satan and later fulfilled in Satan's defeat by the Son. The mysteriousness of this doom does not, as Milton sees it, take away the literal application of the curse, so Satan, as well as the serpent, must be made to move flat upon his belly. This doom could conceivably not be fulfilled until the Last Day, but it suits Milton's purpose much better to have it fulfilled within the limits of his poem. Hence Satan's transformation into a snake in the scene in Hell in Book X. But Milton does more than merely transform him into a snake. He also invents a transformation series for him:

Thus were they plagu'd
And worn with Famin, long and ceasless hiss,
Till thir lost shape, permitted, they resum'd,
Yearly enjoynd, some say, to undergo
This annual humbling certain number'd days,
To dash thir pride, and joy for Man seduc't.
However some tradition they dispers'd
Among the Heathen of thir purchase got,
And Fabl'd how the Serpent, whom they calld
*Ophion* with *Eurynome*, the wide-

Encroaching *Eve* perhaps, had first the rule
Of high *Olympus*, thence by *Saturn* driv'n
And *Ops*, ere yet *Dictaen Jove* was born.
(X, 572-584)

For all the use here of pagan fable Milton's thesis is one arrived at by logical means. For clearly Satan did not after this transformation stay always in serpent kind: he appears before Christ in the wilderness for example in other than serpent shape. So the change in his nature in Book X was not, until after the Last Day, final. And there was reason to suppose that this was not anyway the first time that he had been a serpent since Revelation describes Michael's war against Satan as being a war against the dragon (Revelation 12: 7). This gives Milton warrant for his invention of a process of transformation, and he also characteristically systematizes it. His words 'permitted,' 'certain,' number'd' insist on the ordering power of God in the matter. With all this in mind, the way in which Satan is first presented in the poem is important:

Thus Satan talking to his neerest Mate
With Head up-lift above the wave, and Eyes
That sparkling blaz'd, his other Parts besides
Prone on the Flood, extended long and large
Lay floating many a rood, in bulk as huge
As whom the Fables name of monstrous size . . .
(I, 192-197)

What Milton is describing, as the sparkling eyes (cf. 'brazen Eyes' (VII, 496) and 'Carbuncle his Eyes' (IX, 500) in the descriptions of other serpents) and the proneness show, is the serpent, the sea-dragon, that Satan here in fact is. Satan's first appearance in the poem, like his last, is as the monster.

# 4

# The Satanic Poem

I

THE theme of God's providence thus imposes important logical constraints upon the material of *Paradise Lost*, constraints which are perfectly in harmony with the other important constraints of the poem, those of literary theory and the commitment to write the proper neo-classical poem. But the acceptance of one truth involves the rejection of many sorts of untruth, and very characteristically Milton's awareness of the rightness and appropriateness of his own case goes along with his awareness of the error of other cases. If the growth of a work of art is organic, in accordance with certain principles, then its growth is within limits, within certain degrees of freedom. The sort of development permitted by one set of principles will be excluded by another. Any particular subject can be made into many different sorts of poem. So if a poem has a thesis it can also have a controversy. This opens up an interesting field to the logically minded poet who, as Milton did, likes a quarrel. A tactic of differentiation was made possible, and the adoption of this in *Paradise Lost* is crucial to the nature of the poem. It quite consciously rejects the wrong sort of system, and this rejected system, with its own ideology and literary theory, plays a radical part in the development of the argument. It is quite explicitly and deliberately written into the poem and belongs to the world of Hell. For Milton's devils are poets and thinkers too as this very important account of their activities shows:[1]

> Others more milde,
> Retreated in a silent valley, sing
> With notes Angelical to many a Harp
> Thir own Heroic deeds and hapless Fall
> By doom of Battel; and complain that Fate
> Free Vertue should enthrall to Force or Chance.
> Thir song was partial, but the harmony
> (What could it less when Spirits immortal sing?)
> Suspended Hell, and took with ravishment
> The thronging audience. In discourse more sweet
> (For Eloquence the Soul, Song charms the Sense,)
> Others apart sat on a Hill retir'd,
> In thoughts more elevate, and reason'd high
> Of Providence, Foreknowledge, Will and Fate,
> Fixt Fate, free will, foreknowledg absolute,
> And found no end in wandring mazes lost.
> Of good and evil much they argu'd then,
> Of happiness and final misery,
> Passion and Apathie, and glory and shame,
> Vain wisdom all, and false Philosophie:
> Yet with a pleasing sorcerie could charm
> Pain for a while or anguish, and excite
> Fallacious hope, or arm th'obdured brest
> With stubborn patience as with triple steel.
>
> (II, 546-569)

This shows the sort of fight for which Milton is spoiling, and this intellectual and poetic Hell is something with which the poem is deeply concerned. It is very important that the passage is so beautiful and pathetic, for it thus represents a very typical mode in Milton's poetry. In being so beautiful it is itself not unlike the songs and discourses which it describes: they also have 'ravishment' and 'pleasing sorcerie' and the power to

[1] For a similar account of this passage, see Howard Schultz, *Milton and Forbidden Knowledge* (New York, 1955), pp. 87-95.

'charm.' The passage is quite deliberately written to convey as much attractiveness as possible and is a quite conscious exercise aimed to strike a full warmth and seductiveness of tone. But this poetry is, as Milton makes clear, simply an enchantment, and words such as 'ravishment,' 'pleasing sorcerie' and 'charm' are used advisedly to send out familiar and important signals. For all its beauty of manner, the matter of what the devils sing and say is unreasonable and misleading. They make the wrong hypotheses about the world with which they are faced, and Milton has most carefully selected the things about which they write. The poets of Hell are preoccupied with what are the two most important literary kinds. They are firstly epic poets, and the thesis of satanic epic is self-glorification: they 'sing/Thir own Heroic deeds.' Secondly they are tragic poets whose heroes find their virtue not free but subject to chance ('hapless fall') and fate ('doom of Battel') and who see themselves as grievously trapped in a world of victimization. These poets are hence perplexed, and their perplexity is the same as that which besets the satanic philosophers who are also concerned with and confused about

> Providence, Foreknowledge, Will and Fate,
> Fixt Fate, free will, foreknowledg absolute.
>
> (II, 559-560)

The two things, satanic literature and satanic philosophy, are made to belong to each other. This is a natural enough thing for Milton to do since he was himself as a writer deeply committed to ideological art. So the poets of Hell grapple with philosophical issues, and the philosophers discourse on matters which have literary implications, on tragic matter of 'final misery' and epic matter of 'glory and shame,' in an eloquent way that reconciles them to their situation. But this alleviation is temporary and illusory. Their hopes are 'fallacious,' and the patience to which they submit is 'stubborn,' a word with important religious overtones and suitably applied to beings not amenable to grace and possessing hardened hearts. The whole passage is clearly and deliberately permeated with the Stoic idea, the Stoic sense of destiny and resignation and voluntary exemption from emotion. Milton was sympathetic to many aspects of Stoicism and clearly saw the heroic and tragic possibilities of its attitudes. But it needed to be based on the right things. There was a true Christian stoicism, eg. that of Job, or Mary in *Paradise Regained* (II, 66-108), and a false pagan stoicism (typified here). The second chorus of *Samson* (652-666) establishes most importantly the same distinction.[2]

In this passage therefore Milton is setting up beside his own poem another poem (or poems) which, if he had been a different sort of poet, he might have written on the same subject. The first subject after all to which the satanic philosophers turns is 'Providence,' the theme of *Paradise Lost*. So his poem is to provide the occasion for an ideological and literary encounter. Here again is a tactic common in Milton's poetry. Literary theory is always employed organically in it, setting up one of the controls under which the work develops.[3] It is so much a part of the poem that it is often written explicitly and elaborately into it, making the poem include its own case and justification. The invocations in *Paradise Lost* and the choruses of *Samson* discuss especial problems and characteristics of the poems in which they occur, and from the very beginning of his work Milton had used this self-consciousness about the nature of his poetry to differentiate it from other, less worthy examples of the same genre. Thus *Comus*, being a masque, had to contain songs and Milton uses the occasion to develop an exercise about the right and the wrong sort of lyric. Comus himself, hearing the Lady sing, defines the two types:

> *Com.* Can any mortal mixture of Earths mould
> Breath such Divine inchanting ravishment?

[2] On Renaisance Neo-Stoicism, see Baker, *The Dignity of Man*, pp. 301-312; Merritt Y. Hughes, 'Myself am Hell,' *MP*, LIV (1956), pp. 88-91; Robert Hoopes, *Right Reason in the English Renaissance* (Cambridge, Mass., 1962), pp. 135-145.
[3] For a very useful account of literary theory in Milton, see Ida Langdon, *Milton's Theory of Poetry and Fine Art* (New Haven, 1924).

Sure somthing holy lodges in that brest
And with these raptures moves the vocal air
To testifie his hidd'n residence;
How sweetly did they float upon the wings
Of silence, through the empty-vaulted night
At every fall smoothing the Raven doune
Of darknes till it smil'd: I have oft heard
My mother *Circe* with the Sirens three,
Amidst the flowry-kirtl'd *Naides*
Culling thir potent hearbs, and balefull drugs,
Who as they sung, would take the prison'd soul,
And lap it in *Elysium*, *Scylla* wept,
And chid her barking waves into attention,
And fell *Charybdis* murmur'd soft applause:
Yet they in pleasing slumber lull'd the sense,
And in sweet madnes rob'd it of it self,
But such a sacred, and home-felt delight,
Such sober certainty of waking bliss
I never heard till now.

(243-263)

Milton, making Comus differentiate his mother's songs from
that of the Lady, is outlining a theory about the lyric. Both sorts
of song delight, but Circe's songs merely delight. They 'lull the
sense' in a 'pleasing slumber' of 'sweet madnes' and are thus the
wrong sort of lyric when compared with the Lady's proper
song which communicates reasonable pleasure, being 'sacred'
and possessing 'sober certainty.' The case for the right kind is
made by setting it very close to the wrong. There is some
trickery at work on Milton's part here since Comus's praise is
evoked not by a serious song but by the Lady's slight though
delightful song to Echo. But Milton is indulging in a proper
enough compliment to the Lady Alice by ascribing to her song
the effect which a song about a more serious subject from other
lips would have. And when later she does discourse on the
deeply serious theme of chastity, the effect of her song (if she
had got as far as singing it) would be of the right order:

Yet should I try, the uncontrouled worth
Of this pure cause would kindle my rap't spirits
To such a flame of sacred vehemence,
That dumb things would be mov'd to sympathize . . .

(792-795)

The discrimination, drawn as finely as possible, is between an emotional excitement ('vehemence') that is 'sacred,' and one (Comus's) that is profane.

This particular chain in *Comus* is concerned with the idea of song. The *Ode on the Morning of Christ's Nativity* shows the same technique at work over the field of pastoral. Milton invents a carefully discriminated occasion for the episode of the shepherds:

VIII

The Shepherds on the Lawn,
Or ere the point of dawn,
    Sate simply chatting in a rustick row;
Full little thought they than
That the mighty *Pan*
    Was kindly com to live with them below;
Perhaps their loves, or els their sheep,
Was all that did their silly thoughts so busie keep.

(85-92)

In St Luke's Gospel the shepherds are merely shepherds, but in the *Ode* Milton deliberately makes them into the typical figures of classical pastoral. The fields in which they abide become the conventional 'Lawns,' their thoughts 'silly,' their concerns not merely rural but also amorous. They are put into this world of classical pastoral in order that the appearance of the heavenly host can jolt them all the more violently out of it. The phrase 'mighty *Pan*' is itself part of the same complex. Their spiritual world is also transformed. The phrase deliberately and harshly redefines a pagan idea: what came upon the shepherds was not simply Pan, their Pan, but an altogether different sort of Pan, 'mighty Pan' in fact, coming 'kindly' because he came surprisingly in their own kind (and hence not at all in Pan's kind) as Man.[4] *Lycidas* too must be seen as another attempt at the discriminated pastoral kind.

So, given these careful drawings of the line between the right and the wrong sort of song and the right and wrong sort of pastoral in the earlier work, it is not surprising that *Paradise Lost* should show the same literary self-consciousness. The passage about the devil's songs and discourse in Book II shows what sort of literature belongs to Hell, and Milton knows perfectly well what they would make of his own plot and how differently they would see it. Satan for example presents the matter very characteristically:[5]

> yet not for those
> Nor what the Potent Victor in his rage
> Can else inflict, do I repent or change,
> Though chang'd in outward lustre; that fixt mind
> And high disdain, from sence of injur'd merit,
> That with the mightiest rais'd me to contend,
> And to the fierce contention brought along
> Innumerable force of Spirits arm'd
> That durst dislike his reign, and me preferring,
> His utmost power with adverse power oppos'd
> In dubious Battel on the Plains of Heav'n,
> And shook his Throne. What though the field be lost?
> All is not lost; the unconquerable Will,
> And study of revenge, immortal hate,
> And courage never to submit or yield:
> And what is else not to be overcome?
> That Glory never shall his wrath or might

---

[4] For an opposite interpretation which sees Pan as here identified with and not differentiated from Christ, see Rosamund Tuve, *Images and Themes in Five Poems by Milton* (Cambridge, Mass., and Oxford, 1957), p. 57. But Miss Tuve allows that Pan as a type of Christ was not widely used in art. The glosses to the April and May eclogues of *The Shepheardes Calender* are often quoted in support of seeing Pan as Christ, but the May eclogue also recognizes the possibility of the opposite interpretation ('By whych Pan, though of some be vnderstoode the great Satanas . . . yet I think it more properly meant of the death of Christ').

[5] On Satan as classical hero, see C. M. Bowra, *From Virgil to Milton* (London, 1948), pp. 228-230.

Extort from me. To bow and sue for grace
With suppliant knee, and deifie his power
Who from the terrour of this Arm so late
Douted his Empire, that were low indeed,
That were an Ignominy and shame beneath
This downfall; since by Fate the strength of Gods
And this Empyreal substance cannot fail . . .
(I, 94-117)

This is satanic epic, extravagantly heroic and glamorous. The plot is egotistically pointed up, the concern is for glory and fear of shame, the mind is obdurate, the thought erroneous (eg. the reference to 'Fate'). This account of the plot of *Paradise Lost* contrasts very interestingly with the account of the plot which Satan gives when he reports in Hell the upshot of his mission on Earth:

Him by fraud I have seduc'd
From his Creator, and the more to increase
Your wonder, with an Apple; he thereat
Offended, worth your laughter, hath giv'n up
Both his beloved Man and all his World,
To Sin and Death a prey, and so to us,
Without our hazard, labour, or allarme . . .
(X, 485-491)

What has happened in Book IX turns out on this view to have lacked the epic qualities of danger and struggle, being without 'hazard, labour, or allarme.' And the devils' attitude to the matter of the apple is very like that of Aristotle to the pursuit of Hector as a dramatic subject:[6] possibly marvellous ('to increase/Your wonder') it falls nevertheless into the ridiculous ('worth your laughter').[7] The passage offers a useful pointer to Milton's recognition of the difficulties and problems of his chosen subject, especially with regard to its epic magnitude. It would not, obviously, be Satan's choice.

[6] *Poetics*, trans. Bywater, p. 83.
[7] M. M. Mahood, *Poetry and Humanism* (London, 1950), p. 210, aptly calls it an 'infernal comedy.'

## II

The critical issue between Christian and pagan (or satanic) thought and literature is that of human freedom and responsibility, and this issue bears most importantly upon the centre of *Paradise Lost*. Lacking the sense of God's providence, the devils lack enlightenment when they consider the manner in which their world is disposed. In their view they are subject either to chance or to fate. There is either no system at all, or else they are constrained by the wrong sort of system. It is these two concepts of fate and chance that need to be identified as the ideological enemy in *Paradise Lost*, since they represent the wrong deduction from a set of facts which, rightly interpreted, would lead to the idea of God's providence. This differentiation between Christian and pagan thought was a commonplace of theological writing, on which St Augustine's *City of God* and Boethius' *Consolation of Philosophy* gave important leads. Its use in literature was equally commonplace since it provided a useful ideological way of distinguishing the true from the false, the virtuous from the vicious. Spenser for example finds it helpful in the *Faerie Queene*, Book I, when, the sorcerer Archimago having brought a succubus disguised as Una to the Red Cross Knight's bed, the knight should distinguish his true lady from this false image of her by looking very hard at the way in which this supposed Una talks:

> Ah Sir, my liege Lord and my loue,
> Shall I accuse the hidden cruell fate,
> And mightie causes wrought in heaven aboue,
> Or the blind God, that doth me thus amate,
> For hoped loue to winne me certaine hate?
> Yet thus perforce he bids me do, or die.
> Die is my dew: yet rew my wretched state
> You, whom my hard auenging destinie
> Hath made iudge of my life or death indifferently.
>
> (I, *I*, li)

'Fate,' 'blind God,' 'hard auenging destinie,' indicating a set of beliefs that is radically unChristian, are clues which offer a way of piercing the demon's disguise. So too, when later in the same book Despair discourses to the Red Cross Knight about the way in which the world is ordered:

> Is not his deed, what euer thing is donne,
>     In heauen and earth? did he not all create
>     To die againe? all ends that was begonne.
>     Their times in his eternall book of fate
>     Are written sure, and haue their certaine date.
>     Who then can strive with strong necessitie,
>     That holds the world in his still chaunging state,
>     Or shunne the death ordaynd by destinie?
> When houre of death is come, let none aske whence, nor why.
>
> (I, *IX*, xlii)

the unChristian way in which he uses words like 'fate,' 'necessitie,' and 'destinie' focuses the dangerous nature of his argument. *Arcadia* too, for all its atmosphere of Greek mythology, is at its ideological foundations securely based on the same issue. Basilius' retirement to the country in order to avoid the doom foretold by the oracle illustrates a distrust of providence unseemly in a king: 'wisdom and vertue be the only destinies appointed to man to follow, whence we ought to seeke all our knowledge, since they be such guydes as cannot faile,'[8] and Pamela's important refutation of Cecropia's '*Atheisme*' is also a disquisition on Chance and the immutability of God.[9]

The whole body of Milton's work shows him alive to the differentiation. Writing as a theologian he starts *The Christian Doctrine* by distinguishing God's providence from what non-Christian writers called destiny or fortune (XIV, 27), and as a Christian poet he was also profoundly concerned with the same theme. He presented it often enough with a characteristic

---

[8] *Works*, ed. Feuillerat (Cambridge, 1912), I, 24.
[9] ibid., I, 407-410.

fineness of effect. *Lycidas*, for example, derives much of its massiveness and authority from its being so argumentative and intellectual a poem (the only other elegy in the Memorial volume which adopts the mythological and classical manner— that of Isaac Oliver—shows how flabby that manner can become if it is indulged without concern for its ideological implications) and seeks out the truth about God's providence across a waste of pagan ideological débris. What the pastoral gods lack is a concept of providence: they can neither explain nor protect. The death of Lycidas can by them ultimately be seen only as the process of fate:

> It was that fatall and perfidious bark
> Built in th'eclipse, and rigg'd with curses dark,
> That sunk so low that sacred head of thine.
>
> (100–102)

and Milton deliberately makes the most tragic part of the poem, the vision of the drowned man in the sea, reverberate with the most desolating ideological implications:

> Look homeward Angel now, and melt with ruth,
> And, O ye *Dolphins*, waft the haples youth.
>
> (163–164)

This recourse to the other pagan concept, haplessness or mischance, is weighted by the fact that Lycidas was drowned to the north of Cornwall: the apparently guardian and providential angel, St Michael on his mount, was looking the wrong way, southward to Spain ('Look homeward Angel'). Thus the poem's sudden assertion of a universe of purpose and rationality

> Weep no more, woful Shepherds weep no more
> For *Lycidas* your sorrow is not dead . . .
>
> (165–166)

resolves all the more strikingly the poem's argument about what sort of sense the event makes. The *Ode on the Morning of Christ's Nativity* also deals with the superannuation of an untidy and brutal pagan world by an ordered Christian one. How brilliantly and clearly Milton read the matter can perhaps best be seen in the way he presents the fact that Christ's full glory will be seen at the end even more than at the beginning of his life:

### XVI

But wisest Fate says no,
This must not yet be so,
   The Babe lies yet in smiling Infancy,
That on the bitter cross
Must redeem our loss . . .

(149-153)

The attribute of the Christian God that most differentiates him from the heathen destiny is his providence, so by calling that providence 'wisest Fate' Milton sharpens the issue to as fine a point as possible. His use of 'Fate' here may be likened to Dryden's explication of the word in his letter to William Walsh, providing a detailed critique of the latter's *A Dialogue Concerning Women* (1691). Dryden quotes two lines and comments:

Kind Fate or Fortune, blend them if you can:
And of two wretches make one happy man.
*Kind Fate* looks a little harsh: *Fate* without an epithet is always taken in the ill sense. *Kind* added changes the signification.[10]

The jarring effect which Dryden's 'harsh' implies is precisely what Milton in his phrase in the *Ode* wishes to achieve.

The really distinctive quality in Milton's mind is its capacity to move logically and systematically, and it showed to particular advantage where these questions of differentiation were involved. That was why he found controversy a very appropriate medium of expression. His mind possessed quite extraordinary powers of intellectual diffraction, breaking up an argument or an episode into separate detail. The following extract from the *Doctrine and Discipline of Divorce* shows how

[10] '*Of Dramatic Poesy and Other Critical Essays*,' ed. George Watson, Everyman's Library (London, New York, 1962), II, 54.

fine a mind it is in these respects. Milton is defending his religion from the charge that it makes God the author of sin. The Christian truth, he argues, is that Man is the author of his own sin because Adam's original perfection was in the keeping of his own free will:

> Whenas the doctrine of Plato and Chrysippus with their followers the Academics and the Stoics, who knew not what a consummat and most adorned Pandora was bestow'd upon Adam to be the nurse and guide of his arbitrary happinesse and perseverance, I mean his native innocence and perfection, which might have kept him from being our true Epimetheus, and though they taught of vertue and vice to be both the gift of divine destiny, they could yet find reasons not invalid, to justifie the counsels of God and Fate from the insulsity of mortall tongues: That mans own freewill self-corrupted is the adequat and sufficient cause of his disobedience besides Fate; as Homer also wanted not to express both in his Iliad and Odyssei. And Manilius the Poet, although in his fourth book he tells of some created both to sinne and punishment; yet without murmuring and with an industrious cheerfulnes he acquitts the Deity. They were not ignorant in their heathen lore, that it is most God-like to punish those who of his creatures became his enemies with the greatest punishment; and they could attain also to think that the greatest, when God himselfe throws a man furthest from him; which then they held hee did, when he blinded, hard'n'd, and stirr'd up his offendors to finish, and pile up their disperat work since they had undertak'n it. To banish for ever into a locall hell, whether in the aire or in the center, or in that uttermost and bottomlesse gulph of Chaos, deeper from holy blisse then the worlds diameter multiply'd, they thought not a punishing so proper and proportionat for God to inflict, as to punish sinne with sinne. Thus were the common sort of Gentiles wont to think, without any wry thoughts cast upon divine governance.
>
> (III, Part II, 441-442)

This is a most outstanding exercise, and the line between Christian and pagan argument is drawn with fantastic ingenuity. In so far as Milton is, in respect of his own thesis about

Man's responsibility for sin, anxious to make the alternative thesis as untenable as possible, he designedly allows as much as he can to the pagan viewpoint: the truth, he insists, is so obvious that even the pagans saw it. The points about which the pagans were right were (1) that Man's own free will is responsible for his disobedience ('That man's own free will self corrupted . . .'); (2) that the nature of Man's relationship with God gives no cause for despair ('without murmuring . . .'); (3) that offences against God himself are properly visited with the greatest punishment ('that it is most God-like to punish . . .'); (4) that there is a physical hell ('To banish for ever . . .'); (5) that this physical hell still removes sinners less far from God than sin itself does ('they thought not a punishing so proper . . .'); (6) that God's providence is thus in no way indicted ('without any wry thoughts cast . . .'). But, granting all this, Milton nevertheless carefully marks out those points where the pagans were wrong: (1) they were ignorant about the innocence with which God had in the beginning endowed his creatures ('who knew not what a consummat and most adorned *Pandora* . . .'). This offers an interesting logical development. For in so far as he was given a gift (i.e. his innocence), then Adam was like Epimetheus (who was given Pandora). But if only Adam had made the proper use of the gift of his innocence, then he would have been not at all like Epimetheus, for the gifts which the gods had sent with Pandora were (since Prometheus had angered the gods by stealing their fire from heaven) sent to punish mankind. But God's gift to Adam was a blessing, sent in order to give Adam the wherewithal to make himself very unlike Epimetheus (i.e. happy not miserable). As things turned out Adam did become like Epimetheus because he used his free will to corrupt himself and so brought misery upon mankind. So in that respect the pagan line is again the true one ('our true Epimetheus'). The pagans were also wrong in that (2) their conception of the divine, in so far as it is expressed by such terms as 'destiny' and 'Fate,' is erroneous ('though they taught vertue and vice . . .').

In this careful explication of the myth of Pandora, a complicated argument is superbly steered, and this logical power of the prose is also present in the poetry. The technique adopted in the Pandora passage above can, in its moving by unlikeness and likeness, be paralleled in simile:

> So to the Silvan Lodge
> They came, that like *Pomona*'s Arbour smil'd
> With flourets deck't and fragrant smells; but *Eve*
> Undeckt, save with her self more lovely fair
> Then Wood-Nymph, or the fairest Goddess feign'd
> Of three that in Mount *Ida* naked strove,
> Stood to entertain her guest from Heav'n; no vaile
> Shee needed, Vertue-proof, no thought infirme
> Altered her cheek. On whom the Angel *Haile*
> Bestowd, the holy salutation us'd
> Long after to blest *Marie*, second *Eve*.
>
> (V, 377-387)

Eve, in that she has an arbour decked with flowers, is like Pomona. But unlike the arbours Eve is not decked, for, being naked, she is not adorned at all except that, paradoxically, her very nakedness can be seen as an adornment. In her beauty Eve is supreme, there being no other Roman goddess like her, not even Venus who was judged by Paris to be the fairest goddess of all. Venus is also unlike Eve in that she is mythological whereas Eve is real, a part of Christian history. But Venus can be compared to Eve in that each of them stood naked before someone who was not her husband, Venus before Paris, and Eve before Raphael. But Eve, unlike Venus, stood secure in her virtue. (The idea of a 'thought infirme' altering Venus's cheek is a pleasant sarcasm.) Furthermore, in her entertaining a guest from Heaven Eve is like Mary, blessed too like her, and the visiting angel said 'Haile' to Mary as Raphael here says 'Haile' to Eve. And this likeness of Eve to Mary has a typological significance, for Mary is in that respect a 'second *Eve*.' (It is important that this last Christian comparison of Eve to Mary is developed wholly in terms of its likenesses.)

III

This differentiation between Christian and pagan thinking about providence, destiny and chance has a most important extension in the field of literary theory. Boethius, discussing the issues, had also explicitly defined the nature of tragedy: 'What other thing doth the outcry of tragedies lament, but that fortune, having no respect, overturneth happy states?'[11] The literary kinds had altogether conventional ideologies associated with them, the epic concerned with achievement, the tragic with suffering. The plot was exemplary of some process. When Shakespeare makes tragical matter out of the story of Richard III, he invents Margaret's curse so that events are shaped into the fulfilment of a destiny. Timon likewise is a victim of Fortune's wheel. It was the prerogative of Christian writing that it could always of its very nature rationalize this process, seeing suffering as retributive, and the just as redeemed. Here, Christian literature had the edge on pagan. Sidney for example sees his heroes as being nobler than others for having undertaken their adventures not through involuntary chance or destiny, but freely, out of their own choice and virtue: 'thinking it not so worthy, to be brought to heroycall effects by fortune, or necessitie (like *Ulysses* and *Aeneas*) as by ones owne choice and working.' [12] So the association between satanic philosophy and satanic literature which Milton establishes in his account of the devils in Book II, 546-569 is long standing, and he has a literary as well as an ideological enemy in the poem. This enemy is classical tragedy and epic. That this is indeed the case may easily be established with reference to *Paradise Regained* where Christ's demonstration of the superiority of Christian philosophy over Greek leads also to a demonstration of the corresponding superiority of Christian literature, the Greek tragedians being identified as those who treat (and

---

[11] *Consolation of Philosophy* (Book II, prose II), Loeb Classical Library (London and Cambridge, Mass., 1936), p. 181.
[12] *Arcadia*, ed. Feuillerat, I, 206.

treat erroneously) of 'fate, and chance, and change in human life' (IV, 265). Once again Milton's intelligence is shown in the subtlety and extensiveness with which he develops a common-place enough differentiation. As applied to the epic and the drama it means that any particular episode or plot can be looked at in more than one way so that its implications will differ in the light of the different hypotheses that may be made about it. The tragedy of Samson is a case in point. It can be fitted into either a Christian or a pagan scheme. Milton's sense of this enables him to make a nice point in Harapha's first words to Samson: 'I come not *Samson*, to condole thy chance' (1076). Harapha characteristically sees Samson's plight as a misfortune, part of the world's random way. But he is wrong: Samson's distress is the result not of mischance but of Samson's own sin, a point which Samson has himself learned to acknowledge earlier in the play. Two schemes about the situation are seen as possible, the pagan wrong one (Samson is unlucky) and the Christian right one (his plight is just). Harapha's calling it 'chance' marks his pagan role. The same readings and misreadings come most usefully to hand over the manner in which Samson's death is to be interpreted. Milton has to insist that Samson's decision to destroy the theatre was made in order to kill his enemies and not himself since the latter would be suicide and hence a sin. So, to rule out Samson's will in respect to his own death, Milton plays the suicide off as a satanic tragedy, in the argument prefacing the play as a matter of mischance ('accident'): '*what* Samson *had done to the* Philistins, *and by accident to himself,*' and in the play itself as a matter of fate ('necessity'):

> and now ly'st victorious
> Among thy slain self-kill'd
> Not willingly, but tangl'd in the fold
> Of dire necessity, whose law in death conjoin'd
> Thee with thy slaughter'd foes ...
> (1663-1667)

73

Satan himself in *Paradise Regained* is naturally made to read his situation in the light of his own erroneous hypotheses:

> 'Tis true, I am that Spirit unfortunate,
> Who leagu'd with millions more in rash revolt
> Kept not my happy Station, but was driv'n
> With them from bliss to the bottomless deep . . .
>
> (I, 358-361)

The speech is made to sound very moving, but to see himself as 'unfortunate,' deliberately at the same time generating a warmth of tone on his own behalf (like the devils' song in *Paradise Lost*, Book II, it is 'partial' and takes with 'ravishment'), is an attempt to mislead. Christ, in his reply, reads the situation rightly: 'Deservedly thou griev'st, compos'd of lies/From the beginning' (I, 407-408), seeing Satan's plight as just, a tragedy of wrong but free choice.

These effects are important and subtle in *Paradise Lost*, arising out of the ideological core of the work. The different readings which a situation admits can be very ingeniously played off against each other, making for a sort of ideological punning. God for example uses 'chance' very ironically when he pretends to wonder at Adam's failing to meet him in the garden after the Fall:

> Or come I less conspicuous, or what change
> Absents thee, or what chance detains?
>
> (X, 107-108)

But Adam does not happen simply not to be around, which the use of 'chance' would imply. He is absent by design, being guilty and ashamed, something which God knows perfectly well. An equally nice tension is set up by the use of 'occasion' about Raphael's visit to the Garden: 'sudden mind arose/In *Adam*, not to let th'occasion pass' (V, 452-453). As Adam sees it, the visit is indeed an 'occasion' (an event that has unexpectedly befallen): Raphael has just happened to drop in without notice and without their having any expectation of his coming.

74

But in the heavenly dimension Raphael's visit is not in this sense an occasion at all: he is there by design, being sent by God in order to warn and exhort Adam and Eve about their responsibility and obedience.

These are all cases where one situation can be looked at in contrasting ways. Equally certain words can be read differently according to the hypotheses with which they are associated. Words such as 'nature,' 'free,' 'lot,' 'doom' are words whose implications can vary according to the ideological context in which they are used. 'Doom,' for example, in the Christian context means the will or decree of God, as when Eve refers to the forbidden Fruit: 'In the day we eate/Of this fair Fruit, our doom is, we shall die' (IX, 762-763). 'Doom' here is simply judgment. On the other hand in the satanic context, 'hapless fall/By doom of Battel' (II, 549), the word is clearly associated with fate, something that conspires against the free spirit.

This technique of differentiation, philosophical and literary, plays an important part in the argument of *Paradise Lost*. Opposed to the true thesis of God's providence are the two satanic theses of chance and fate. These are the intellectual co-ordinates of the poem. They make for a quite conscious complexity and provide the occasion for an elaborate logical exercise. It is here that the poem differs from the treatise on Christian doctrine. The latter has only the doctrine and the differentiation of the true from the false, but the poem has, beyond that, a shrewd manipulation of the ideologies with regard to each other.

# 5

# 'Hapless Eve'

## I

THE account of the Fall is based on Genesis:

8 And the LORD God planted a garden eastward in Eden; and there he put the man whom he had formed.
9 And out of the ground made the LORD God to grow every tree that is pleasant to the sight, and good for food; the tree of life also in the midst of the garden, and the tree of knowledge of good and evil.
16 And the LORD God commanded the man, saying, Of every tree of the garden thou mayest freely eat:
17 But of the tree of the knowledge of good and evil, thou shalt not eat of it: for in the day that thou eatest thereof thou shalt surely die.
18 And the LORD God said, It is not good that the man should be alone; I will make him an help meet for him.

(Genesis 2)

NOW the serpent was more subtil than any beast of the field which the LORD God had made. And he said unto the woman, Yea, hath God said, Ye shall not eat of every tree of the garden?
2 And the woman said unto the serpent, We may eat of the fruit of the trees of the garden:
3 But of the fruit of the tree which is in the midst of the garden, God hath said, Ye shall not eat of it, neither shall ye touch it, lest ye die.

4 And the serpent said unto the woman, Ye shall not surely die:
5 For God doth know that in the day ye eat thereof, then your
eyes shall be opened, and ye shall be as gods, knowing good and
evil.
6 And when the woman saw that the tree was good for food, and
that it was pleasant to the eyes, and a tree to be desired to make
one wise, she took of the fruit thereof, and did eat, and gave also
unto her husband with her; and he did eat.
7 And the eyes of them both were opened, and they knew that
they were naked; and they sewed fig leaves together, and made
themselves aprons.

(Genesis 3)

This account can be either condensed or expanded. It is for
example much more complicated than the way in which the
Fall is looked at in Heaven. In that dimension we are given a
much simpler tidier account, God's version of the Fall in Book
III does not for instance differentiate between Adam and Eve:

> Man falls deceiv'd
> By the other first: Man therefore shall find grace,
> The other none . . .
>
> (III, 130-132)

That it was Eve not Adam who was deceived by Satan is
irrelevant here: 'Man' is used to include both Adam and Eve.
Michael at the end of the poem also adopts the radical and
simple divine view:

> *Adam*, now ope thine eyes, and first behold
> Th'effects which thy original crime hath wrought
> In some to spring from thee, who never touch'd
> Th'excepted Tree, nor with the Snake conspir'd,
> Nor sinn'd thy sin . . .
>
> (XI, 423-427)

But 'touch' was a word that was associated with Eve and not
Adam (Genesis 3: 3), nor had Adam conspired with the snake.
　　But clearly the Genesis account was more often expanded.
It was seen to imply more than it stated. In the first place it

showed the various ways in which God's providence might manifest itself. That providence was obviously good since it provided so extensively for Adam's welfare by setting him in a beautiful garden, giving him good food and by making a wife for him. It was protective since it warned Adam not to eat the forbidden Fruit. It was also remedial since it created Eve in order to prevent Adam's being lonely. The remedial aspect of God's providence plays a very important part in Milton's explication of the Fall, and it is sometimes misinterpreted. It enables Milton to set up certain arrangements which might not at first sight seem good but which turn out to be no indictment of God's providence since God has provided against them. Thus Adam's speech to God about his loneliness seems to expand Genesis at some risk:

> Thou in thyself art perfet, and in thee
> Is no deficience found; not so is Man,
> But in degree, the cause of his desire
> By conversation with his like to help,
> Or solace his defects. No need that thou
> Shouldst propagat, already infinite;
> And through all numbers absolute, though One;
> But Man by number is to manifest
> His single imperfection, and beget
> Like of his like, his Image multipli'd,
> In unitie defective, which requires
> Collateral love, and deerest amitie.
>
> (VIII, 415-426)

but the words 'deficience,' 'defects,' 'imperfection,' 'defective' here argue no failure in God's providence since God will, in the provision of a wife, give remedy and solace to Adam. On this view it would be perfectly provident for God to provide a vehicle with wheels and an incline for it to run down so long as he also fitted it with a steering wheel and brakes.

In the second place the Genesis account was seen to make for some difficulty, and the problems could be seen as the result of omission and compression. The apparently isolated act of

Genesis must have been the outcome of a process. The serpent's 'Yea' (3 : 1) would seem to indicate that the story began in what was actually the middle of a dialogue. The moral issue was seen also to be more complex than Genesis apparently allowed. Ames for example quite properly pointed out that something very relevant but omitted from Genesis must have preceded the actual eating of the fruit: '6. The committing of the transgression was accomplished in the eating of the forbidden Fruit, which was called the Tree of the knowledge of *good* and *Evill*: but the first motion or degree of this disobedience, did necessarily goe before that outward act of eating, so that it may truly be said that Man was a sinner, before he had finished that outward act of eating.'[1] The important problems that Genesis was seen to raise were these: (1) Was Eve alone when the serpent was talking to her? (2) What did Eve know about the forbidden Tree, since God's injunction not to eat it is made to Adam alone. (3) Does it matter that Genesis says nothing about the real tempter, i.e. that it was Satan making use of the serpent? (4) What was the nature of the forbidden Tree? (5) What was the process of Adam's fall? So the most necessary expansion of Genesis was to develop it so as to solve these problems in ways that made the story compatible with the idea of a provident God.

So there was much warrant for an expansion of Genesis and, since the whole of *Paradise Lost* has to do with the Fall, Milton's expansion of the story is massive.[2] But it all goes back to that simple centre and to the simple central theme. Starting with the Fall and its problems, Milton worked his way outward, into Book IX and beyond that into the rest of the poem. He was working to establish a situation in which the Fall could occur without God's providence being indicted. Thus, although the episodes of the poem have various sorts of interest—human and poetic since they are moving and

---

[1] William Ames, *The Marrow of Sacred Divinity* (1642), p. 56.

[2] Sims, *The Bible in Milton's Epics*, p. 41, makes the interesting point that Book IX includes fewer allusions to the Bible than do some of the other books of the poem.

beautiful—they are also fitted into a logical scheme.[3] They exemplify God's providence. The episodes before Book IX are not absolutely necessary inventions as those of Book IX itself are: Eve, for example, did not have to see her reflection in the pool (Book IV) whereas she did have to be found alone in the Garden (Book IX). But they provide a series of useful and instructive incidents, providing warning and remedy for Adam and Eve, and, for the reader, instruction and delight and important leads on how the Fall itself has to be read. It follows, since they are intended to help and not to hinder the poem's thesis, that they must not be interpreted in such a way as to show that Adam and Eve are already fallen creatures before Book IX is reached.[4]

II

The first important episode in Book IX is the separation of Adam and Eve. Genesis does not say whether Eve was alone or not when she was talking with the serpent but most of the commentators argued, logically enough, that she was, since the speciousness of the serpent's arguments would have been immediately apparent to Adam. Eve's reproaches to Adam after their Fall show how nicely Milton measured this problem:

> Imput'st thou that to my default, or will
> Of wandring, as thou call'st it, which who knows
> But might as ill have happ'nd thou being by,
> Or to thy self perhaps: hadst thou been there,
> Or here th'attempt, thou couldst not have discernd
> Fraud in the Serpent, speaking as he spake . . .
>
> (IX, 1145-1150)

[3] For other accounts of these episodes and the argument, see especially Diekhoff, *Paradise Lost: a Commentary on the Argument*; and Joseph H. Summers, *The Muse's Method: an Introduction to Paradise Lost* (Cambridge, Mass., and London, 1962). My own approach has a different emphasis and differs in detail.

[4] See especially, Millicent Bell, 'The Fallacy of the Fall in *Paradise Lost*,' *PMLA*, LXVIII (1953), 863-883.

But Adam would not have fallen if he had met and been tempted by Satan on his own: Satan makes it clear that he shuns Adam's 'higher intellectual' and moral strength (IX, 483). And if Adam had been with Eve when she was tempted he would likewise not have allowed her to be deceived. Eve's claim in her speech that her meeting with the serpent was an unfortunate happening ('as ill have happ'nd'), a description made deliberately redolent of the satanic ideology of mischance, points to Milton's awareness of all the wrong implications of the event. If Eve's being found alone is simply her bad luck, then the poem's thesis that God is provident breaks down. The poem would be satanic not Christian tragedy. So there are important limiting conditions upon Eve's being alone. She must be alone by decision and not accident, and also with Adam's acquiescence. For if Adam does not condone her going, then he will have no involvement whatever in her fall, in which case the divine view that does not differentiate between Adam and Eve (III, 130) would be unjust. Their separation thus has to be brought about by some careful invention.

Other literary treatments of Genesis saw no difficulty in getting Eve alone. Joseph Beaumont in *Psyche* simply calls it an 'Unhappy Error' and makes the act of parting Eve's doing.[5] Some writers invent episodes. The *Adamo Caduto* has a very pretty invention in which Adam, just after his marriage to Eve, is lured away by an echo that passes musically through the Garden.[6] But this is the sort of invention whose logical implications have to be very carefully looked at. It leaves Eve's being found alone still a problem, a matter either of her bad luck or else of Adam's bad judgment or inadvertence. But the former does not implicate Adam, and the latter (bad judgment or inadvertence) is too important for it to be merely deduced by the reader. Vondel does see the element of chance in the

[5] Canto VI, st. 271. (*Works*, ed. G. B. Grosart, Chertsey Worthies' Library (1880), I, 115).

[6] Act II, sc. V. See Kirkconnell, *The Celestial Cycle*, p. 315.

episode. In his *Adam in Ballingschap* Belial, proposing to tempt Eve, hopes that Eve might 'happen' to be found on her own, and Asmodeus takes this up:

> Fortune agrees to this: the huntsman's art
> Is still dependent upon time and place
> And nature's disposition.[7]

Vondel uses the right terms—'happen,' 'Fortune'[8]—but fails to see the disastrous implications which they have in the light of God's providence. The element of responsibility is crucial to Eve's encounter with the serpent. Milton's God had before Book IX laid down the important condition that Man's happiness was 'in his power left free to will' (V, 235), indicating that Man's world was as little 'satanic' as his own where 'Necessitie and Chance/Approach not mee, and what I will is Fate' (VII, 172-173). Furthermore Adam had necessarily to be implicated in Eve's fall.

There was an easy and important solution of this to hand. The involvement of Adam and Eve with each other, an involvement so close that the heavenly dimension of the poem does not (when it considers the Fall) differentiate one from the other, could be explicated with reference to the oneness of a man and his wife that marriage established.[9] A relationship that contributed to the human interest of the poem also contributed to its logic. Shakespeare after all had seen that the union could be so close as to make for paradox:

> Property was thus appalled
> That the self was not the same:
> Single nature's double name
> Neither two nor one was called.
>
> Reason, in itself confounded,
> Saw division grow together,

---

[7] ibid., p. 456.

[8] The words of the original are *gelucken, geluck*.

[9] Stein, *Answerable Style*, pp. 78-80, 100-110 and Summers, *The Muse's Method*, pp. 96-97 also discuss this especially close way in which Adam and Eve are part of each other.

To themselves yet either neither,
Simple were so well compounded:

That it cried, How true a twain
Seemeth this concordant one!
Love hath reason, reason none,
If what parts can so remain.
                    ('The Phoenix and Turtle')

The most vital element in this interdependence was the concept
of the helpmeet: '18 And the LORD God said, It is not good
that the man should be alone; I will make him an help meet for
him' (Genesis 2). This concept is importantly dramatized in the
scene after the creation of Eve which is recounted by Eve herself to Adam in Book IV, and followed up in Adam's talk with
Raphael in Book VIII. Eve, when she first wakes after her
creation, goes to the pool and, gazing into it, is taken with the
desire for her own reflection:

                    there I had fixt
     Mine eyes till now, and pin'd with vain desire,
     Had not a voice thus warnd me, What thou seest,
     What there thou seest fair Creature is thy self,
     With thee it came and goes: but follow me,
     And I will bring thee where no shadow staies
     Thy coming, and thy soft imbraces, hee
     Whose image thou art, him thou shall enjoy
     Inseparablie thine, to him shalt beare
     Multitudes like thy self, and thence be call'd
     Mother of human Race . . .
                              (IV, 465-475)

What Eve feels here is not vanity. It is like vanity in that her
love is directed to herself and not to another (and the scene
thus looks forward in some respects to her fall), but vanity
must deliberately reject other forms of love whereas this is the
first and only love that Eve has known. The tone of God's
voice as he addresses her shows that her feeling is in no way
blameworthy. What Eve is experiencing is a need of her

nature but one which needs to be directed to its proper end. God, creating the need, has providentially arranged for its satisfaction since a frustrated desire would be a satanic thing. This latter is imaged for example in the desires (cf. 'jealousie/ . . . the injur'd Lovers Hell' (V, 449-450) ) of Hell which characteristically pine 'Still unfulfill'd with pain of longing' (IV, 511). In this scene at the pool Milton makes Eve subject to that loneliness which Genesis makes Adam only subject to. But Milton sees the loneliness and the provision as working both ways. Adam is a helpmeet for her just as Genesis says that she is for him. And in showing that Eve is capable of error as to where her true good lies, Milton makes the point as to how necessary to her a helpmeet is. At the pool her helpmeet is God who instructs her about the nature of her relationship with Adam. So, when Adam first meets her, he recognizes, as he tells Raphael, that she is informed 'Of nuptial Sanctitie and marriage Rites' (VIII, 487) and he lays claim to her also in terms of the institution:

> I now see
> Bone of my Bone, Flesh of my Flesh, my Self
> Before me; Woman is her Name, of Man
> Extracted; for this cause he shall forgoe
> Father and Mother, and to his Wife adhere;
> And they shall be one Flesh, one Heart, one Soule.
> (VIII, 494-499)

Typically, given his concern for human responsibility, Milton builds up an extraordinary self-consciousness in his characters about their nature and function and, given also his concern for divine providence, shows how that providence is manifested in the institution of a rational and systematized relationship. True marriage consists in the understanding as well as in the playing out of the proper role.

It is in order to establish the full propriety of their marriage that Milton invents the apparently strange episode of Eve's turning away from Adam when she first sees him, his image

84

being at first sight less attractive to her than her own in the
pool (IV, 479). It causes some little local difficulty since Adam
has necessarily not to be offended by it, and he is made to
ascribe it to a proper bashfulness on Eve's part (VIII, 500-503).
But what Milton establishes with the episode is that since
Adam proceeded to follow her and of his own will claimed her
as his wife, and since Eve, when she heard his plea, accepted him
as her husband, their marriage was based on consent which was
a necessary part of marriage (see *Tetrachordon*, IV, 105-106).
They did not marry each other merely because there was no
one else for either of them to get married to. Even though
there was only one man and one woman, there was still
freedom and choice in their coming together. God is not
compelling them to each other. Milton, very aware of the
wrong readings of his matter, is with this small incident
exorcizing the satanic idea of necessity.

The whole episode is thus invented specifically with a
view to what happens in Book IX. Dramatizing the idea of the
helpmeet and defining the institution of marriage, it shows
Eve's capacity for error, her need for instruction. These things
argue no deficiency in her happiness, nor improvidence in God.
Since clearly she did according to Genesis fall into error, she
must necessarily have been made with the capacity for it.
Adam is the helpmeet who will provide reason and authority.
And Eve's incapacity shows that that authority in Adam is
not arbitrary but is itself reasonable. In *Tetrachordon* (IV, 76-77),
dealing with harder, post-lapsarian cases, Milton argues that a
man should submit to his wife where the wife is the more
intelligent partner. Marriage is rational.

III

So Adam, before Book IX, is—as he is not in Genesis—
provided with a warning espisode about Eve's incapacity when
left to herself, and about his own role in providing against it.
Milton is setting up a situation which offers the best logical fit

for Satan's finding Eve alone. The actual circumstances of their separation depend upon the same logical rigorousness. If Eve is found alone, then it must be because she wanted to be alone and because Adam permitted it. Hence Milton's invention of the discussion between them about their gardening apart. The logical constraints insist not merely upon the provision of the episode but also upon much of the way in which it is developed. Since the suggestion that they should work apart turns out to be such a disastrous one, it cannot be Adam's. Also it has not to be absurd, since an intelligent Adam could not agree to it if it were. The proposal is thus made by Eve. She cannot have an evil motive in making it, and Milton prefaces the discourse by indicating that it is provoked by a seemly care to obey God's command that they should tend the Garden:

> Then commune how that day they best may ply
> Thir growing work: for much thir work outgrew
> The hands dispatch of two Gardning so wide . . .
>
> (IX, 201-203)

Eve begins by putting the point about the Garden's wildness very strongly:

> *Adam*, well may we labour still to dress
> This Garden, still to tend Plant, Herb and Flour,
> Our pleasant task enjoyn'd, but till more hands
> Aid us, the work under our labour grows,
> Luxurious by restraint; what we by day
> Lop overgrown, or prune, or prop, or bind,
> One night or two with wanton growth derides
> Tending to wilde.
>
> (IX, 205-212)

Eve is not ignorant of the connection between the garden's wildness and God's injunction to the human pair to multiply and so provide assistance for their labour. Adam had linked the two things together in his speech to Eve about the garden in Book IV, 623-632, but, he now points out to Eve, this does not imply that the interim period will be difficult:

86

For not to irksom toile, but to delight
He made us, and delight to Reason joyn'd.
These paths & Bowers doubt not but our joynt hands
Will keep from Wilderness with ease, as wide
As we need walk, till younger hands ere long
Assist us . . .

(IX, 242-247)

Agreeing that a short separation might be tolerable and possible, he is nevertheless properly possessed by doubt lest their foe take the occasion slyly to assault them, a doubt suitably inspired by Raphael's warning visit: 'thou knowst/ What hath bin warn'd us' (IX, 252-253). Adam has clearly also learned the lesson provided by the episode of Eve's error at her awakening. The matter so far is a model of what Adam's role should be:

leave not the faithful side
That gave thee being, still shades thee and protects.
The Wife, where danger or dishonour lurks,
Safest and seemliest by her Husband staies,
Who guards her, or with her the worst endures.

(IX, 265-269)

Adam's advice is characteristically buttressed by a justification of his right to give advice. The action unfolds within a very theoretical context. Adam here is properly the helpmeet and reminds Eve of the institution by which they live. Milton's own comment about Adam's speech emphasizes this: 'So spake domestick *Adam* in his care/And Matrimonial Love' (IX, 318-319), the attribute 'domestick' pointing to Adam's matrimonial and familial role. So far Adam is made to demonstrate the perfect decorum of a husband, fit subject for a moral and neo-classic art.

Adam's fear lest she meet Satan is used by Eve to forward her second argument for their separating, one concerned with the meaningfulness of a happiness and an integrity which are thus hedged about with restriction:

How are we happie, still in fear of harm? . . .
And what is Faith, Love, Vertue unassaid
Alone, without exterior help sustaind?
Let us not then suspect our happie State
Left so imperfet by the Maker wise,
As not secure to single or combin'd.
Fraile is our happiness, if this be so . . .

(IX, 326 . . . 335-340)

If Eve's first argument about the Garden's wildness is reputable
(though wrongly applied) because it was concerned with an
issue raised earlier in the poem by Adam, this second argument
is reputable because it is concerned with an issue raised in
another context by Milton himself. Insisting on a virtue that
flourishes by trial, Eve uses the argument of *Areopagitica*
against the 'fugitive and cloister'd virtue' (IV, 311). Two points
need to be made about this. Firstly Milton has, by earlier
episodes in the poem, done his best to show that these arguments do not apply to Eve's case.[10] She had erred when on
her own before, and the refutation of her case here is helped
especially by our knowledge of its tragic outcome. Moreover
Eve has begun her argument badly, for her question 'How are
we happie still in fear of harm?' indicts God's providence as
Adam is quick to point out:

O Woman, best are all things as the will
Of God ordain'd them, his creating hand
Nothing imperfet or deficient left
Of all that he Created . . .

(IX, 343-346)

The address 'O Woman' is an important pointer to the line
that Milton is following. It is not cold and aloof but points
instead to the relationship instituted between man and woman.
The theory of marriage again puts the best sense on the
matter. The liberty which Eve claims is not that liberty which
her female nature was created to have.

[10] See John S. Diekhoff, 'Eve, the Devil and Areopagitica,' *M.L.Q*, V (1944),
429-434 for a demonstration of the inapplicability of the argument to Eve's case.

Nevertheless it is at this point that Milton's account of the Fall gets into trouble. Adam, though he rightly denies the relevance of Eve's argument to the issue actually in hand, does finally consent to her departure. For all his perceptiveness, an element of persuasion is involved in the matter. His rationality is at fault since he is overcome by an argument and not a passion. But if God in his providence made Adam wise, it is hard to see how Adam's judgment could fail in any way at all. St Paul rightly saw that Adam could not have been deceived at the moment when he ate the Fruit: '14 And Adam was not deceived, but the woman being deceived was in the transgression' (I Timothy 2), and Adam likewise should not have been deceived here either. It is necessary therefore for Milton to use some sleight of hand in order not to make Adam's intellectual failure seem too blatant. This is the second point that has to be made about Eve's use of the argument from *Areopagitica*. Milton wants to give Eve a very strong-seeming case and very characteristically has recourse to one of his own. He wants a powerful argument for Eve in order not to make Adam look a fool. That many readers of *Paradise Lost* are convinced by Eve's argument measures Milton's success. But the power of her argument is not aimed at justifying her action but rather at mitigating the failure of Adam to see through it. It is important too that for all Eve's reasons Milton still makes Adam intelligent enough to make a very good estimate of the sort of thing that might happen to her on her own, that she might 'fall into deception unaware' (IX, 362). Adam's reluctance too is even more strongly marked than his consent. But for all his intelligence and shrewdness, he does let her go. And that, in the light of what happened, was an unreasonable act.

Genesis provided Milton with the basis for his handling of the episode. When God judges Adam he says: '17 . . . Because thou hast hearkened unto the voice of thy wife, and hast eaten of the tree, of which I commanded thee, saying, Thou shalt not eat of it: cursed is the ground for thy sake . . .' (Genesis 3).

This hearkening to the voice of his wife on Adam's part would normally be taken as a reference to what happened when he ate the forbidden Fruit. In *The Christian Doctrine* Milton argues that amongst the things comprehended in the Fall were '. . . in the man excessive uxuriousness, in the woman a want of proper regard for her husband' (XV, 183), and looking simply at the Genesis account one would suppose that Eve's want of proper regard for her husband was shown in her giving the Fruit also to him after she had herself eaten of the forbidden Tree, and that Adam's excessive uxuriousness was shown in his presumably doting acceptance of the Fruit from her hand. That is as far as a commentary on Genesis could go since that is as far as Genesis itself goes. This is indeed the account which Milton's God himself gives in his judgment after the Fall when he rejects Adam's attempt to blame Eve ('She gave me of the Tree, and I did eate' (X, 143) ):

> Was shee thy God, that her thou didst obey
> Before his voice, or was shee made thy guide,
> Superior, or but equal, that to her
> Thou didst resigne thy Manhood, and the Place
> Wherein God set thee above her made of thee . . .
>
> (X, 145-149)

This account is severely censured by Waldock who regards it as a travesty of what really happened at the Fall and as an attempt to establish a misleading 'official' view of the business.[11] But this is to miss the point. God's view is necessarily the 'official' view since it is necessarily based on what Genesis says. But *Paradise Lost* is an expansion of Genesis: Book IX presents a process, a series of actions. And the 'official' view turns out to apply much more appositely to Milton's invented than to his inherited material. Eve's want of proper regard for her husband lies not merely in her giving him the Fruit but also in her not taking his advice not to stray from his side, and Adam's uxuriousness not only in his eating the Fruit when

[11] *Paradise Lost and its Critics*, p. 50.

it was offered to him but also in his yielding to his wife's arguments that they should garden separately. Eve's recriminations to Adam after the Fall show for example that Adam's hearkening to the voice of his wife is shown rather in this earlier episode of their separation:

> Too facil then thou didst not much gainsay,
> Nay didst permit, approve, and fair dismiss.
> Hadst thou bin firm and fixt in thy dissent,
> Neither had I transgress'd, nor thou with mee.
> (IX, 1158-1161)

Eve is right: Adam's crucial misjudgment was to approve (despite some gainsaying) her departure from him. And if Adam's making any sort of misjudgment argues some deficiency in the story, then it is best that it be deficient here where the question of the Fall, which might be expected to have something directly to do with the forbidden Fruit, seems hardly involved. Milton is doing his best to arrange that such deficiencies as there are in his account are not concerned with the actual eating of the apple. But the episode is none the less vital, and the separation of Adam and Eve the first necessary stage in the process of their Fall.

The discussion between Adam and Eve is thus managed with a great deal of care for its relevance and implications. How carefully Milton is looking at the matter is shown in the comments which he provides about the various speeches:

> And *Eve* first to her Husband thus began. (204)

> To whom mild answer *Adam* thus return'd. (226)

> To whom the Virigin Majestie of *Eve*,
> As one who loves, and some unkindness meets,
> With sweet austeer composure thus reply'd. (270-272)

> To whom with healing words *Adam* replyd. (290)

> So spake domestick *Adam* in his care
> And Matrimonial Love; but *Eve*, who thought
> Less attributed to her Faith sincere,
> Thus her reply with accent sweet renewd. (318-321)

To whom thus *Adam* fervently repli'd. (342)

So spake the Patriarch of Mankinde, but *Eve*
Persisted, yet submiss, though last, repli'd. (376-377)

The scene is often referred to as a quarrel, but these comments
show that this is to read it the wrong way. An unfallen pair
cannot quarrel, and so Milton's comments are intended to keep
the episode on the right lines. His description of Adam after
the Fall as 'first incenst' (IX, 1162) shows that Adam is not
(and cannot be) incensed here. As an exercise in discriminating
between a fallen quarrel and an unfallen difference of opinion
the matter doubtless had some logical appeal for Milton. His
insistence at the close that Eve 'Persisted, yet submiss, though
last, repli'd' (307) is equally careful. Eve, having the last
word, looks totally feminine. But although she has the last
word, being unfallen, she has it with a difference. It is not that,
though seeming submissive, she still managed to have the last
word, but that, though having the last word, she still managed
to stay submissive.

Those last words clinch Adam's involvement in her fall:

With thy permission then, and thus forewarnd
Chiefly by what thy own last reasoning words
Touchd onely, that our trial, when least sought,
May finde us both perhaps farr less prepar'd,
The willinger I goe, nor much expect
A Foe so proud will first the weaker seek . . .
(IX, 378-383)

She is warned, yet still nourishes the erroneous desire to go
('the willinger I goe'). So far she is responsible, but she goes,
as she starts out by saying, with Adam's 'permission.' It is an
important reservation. Eve is not, having wheedled permission
from Adam for her going, now maddeningly loading him
with the responsibility for what she does. Without Adam's
permission she will not go. Wilfulness on her part here would
exonerate Adam. By granting his permission Adam becomes

involved in what happens to her. He is at this point no true
helpmeet. Dryden, in his operatic adaptation of *Paradise Lost*,
provides an interesting example of a very poor reading of
the case. Failing to see how necessary Eve's submission is to the
logic of the matter, he omits it, making her last words simply:

> My soul, my eyes delight, in this I find
> Thou lov'st, because to love is to be kind.[12]

In the interest of a local romantic effect he sacrifices the logic.
His Eve becomes not merely gushing but also wilful, and
the episode loses that coherence with the theme that it has in
*Paradise Lost*.

## IV

Satan's interpretation of his finding Eve alone shows why
Milton has had to go so carefully. In the characteristic way of
his ideology Satan is, in the Garden, taking a chance, running
his luck. On his first visit he had scoured Paradise in the same
haphazard way: 'A chance but chance may lead where I may
meet/Some wandring Spirit of Heav'n' (IV, 530-531). Chance
on that occasion did exactly that, but it was Satan's bad luck
and not his good since it led him straight into the arms of the
angelic guard. That capture of Satan itself provided a useful
illustration of God's providence: it showed that it was not
because he could not stop him that God allowed Satan in
Book IX to approach Adam and Eve. Returned to the garden
then, trying his luck a second time, Satan looks for the serpent,
his chosen means, in the same chance-ridden way, looks 'where
hap may finde/The Serpent sleeping' (IX, 160-161). Satan's
words—'chance,' 'hap'—indicate his belief in a universe of no
pattern, a random world. Thus his sudden encounter with
Eve is, as he sees it, the most colossal piece of luck:

> Then let me not pass
> Occasion which now smiles, behold alone

12 *State of Innocence*, IV, i.

The Woman, opportune to all attempts,
Her Husband, for I view far round, not nigh . . .
(IX, 479-482)

'Occasion,' 'opportune,' are the technical terms of Satan's ideology, used of events that occur without design, that simply happen. But this sort of luck, good for him, would be bad for Eve. That is why Milton has had to provide inventions, episodes that make Eve's being alone spring out of decision. Knowing nothing of Adam's responsibility in the matter, Satan sees the event as one brought about by good fortune. This is to read it in the unprovidential way. Milton, with a steady gaze on all the right and wrong implications of the event, keeps his poem on the true Christian lines and off the wrong satanic ones. Miss Millicent Bell's account of the poem for example falters here. Not liking the way in which Milton brought about the separation of Adam and Eve, she argues that Eve's meeting with Satan 'might have happened quite innocently and accidentally.'[13] But this is precisely how a poem about God's providence cannot let it happen: accident would not be innocent. It is difficult to think of arrangements other than Milton's that would better meet the case.

The literary constraints of the poem are very important. Milton is interested in what sort of tragic event this encounter of Satan and Eve is. He has to make it a tragedy of responsibility, a just and not an unjust event. Satan, the apostle of randomness, reads it wrongly. But Milton is perfectly aware that it can be read very close to Satan's way and still be read rightly. He himself quite deliberately runs this interpretation of the matter in his comments on Eve's parting from Adam:

> O much deceav'd, much failing, hapless *Eve*,
> Of thy presum'd return! event perverse!
> Thou never from that houre in Paradise
> Foundst either sweet repast, or sound repose;
> Such ambush hid among sweet Flours and Shades

---

[13] 'The Fallacy of the Fall etc.,' *PMLA*, LXVIII, 870.

Waited with hellish rancour imminent
To intercept thy way, or send thee back
Despoild of Innocence, of Faith, of Bliss.

(IX, 404-411)

and in his description of Satan's finding Eve alone:

Eve separate he spies,
Veild in a Cloud of Fragrance, where she stood,
Half spi'd, so thick the Roses bushing round
About her glowd, oft stooping to support
Each Flour of slender stalk, whose head though gay
Carnation, Purple, Azure, or spect with Gold,
Hung drooping unsustaind, them she upstaies
Gently with Mirtle band, mindless the while,
Her self, though fairest unsupported Flour,
From her best prop so farr, and storm so nigh.

(IX, 424-433)

Milton, consciously writing up and feeling the pathos of Eve's situation, allowing it to generate a warmth and tenderness of tone, brings his tragedy deliberately close to a tragedy of mischance. He calls Eve 'hapless' (IX, 404). He movingly stresses Eve's exposedness before Satan, her unawareness of danger: 'mindless the while' (IX, 431). Things turned out unexpectedly for her: 'event perverse' (IX, 405) is quite designedly Milton's phrase for Aristotle's peripety, an episode that turns out contrary to intention. But (as always with this especially romantic tone in Milton) it is no mere emotional luxury. This sympathetic note can be struck here because in a very real way this is what the tragedy of Eve is like. Satan, seeing it this way, sees it wrongly because he knows nothing of Adam's responsibility for her being alone. The reader, who does know that, can properly feel pity for Eve. The one person who could not see the episode this way would be Adam. Eve's tragedy of mischance is his tragedy of responsibility. Eve, being genuinely and designedly the weaker of the human pair, being here more helpless in a very real sense,

95

can justly be seen as 'hapless' when she is found alone, but God's providence is not called into question since God has made Adam to be her guide and help. The tragedy is more his failure than hers. The lines

> Her self, though fairest unsupported Flour,
> From her best prop so farr, and storm so nigh.
>
> (IX, 432-433)

are theoretical as well as poetic. They are a metaphorical representation of the idea of the absent helpmeet.

Thus this particular episode of *Paradise Lost* is a logical invention provided in order to insist that the story of the Fall does make sense in terms of God's providence. The closer Milton gets to the Fall, the more does what might well have happened become what must have happened. Eve must have been alone, but to my knowledge only Milton saw the necessity of making Adam responsible for that. He is one of the most intelligent of Biblical commentators. There is no point in wondering whether Adam and Eve were always to stay together like Siamese twins. The logic of the case simply demands that the crucial hour shall find them in a situation which is of their own choosing. Eve, after all, has been on her own before when she left Adam and Raphael to talk together in Book VIII (44). But this is not the sort of time that Satan will be permitted to come upon her. Milton was helped too to get the matter right by his sense of the way in which other writers would have got it wrong. The episode makes for many sorts of tragedy, each with its own framework of implication and justification. *Paradise Lost* is the work of a literary critic as well as a commentator, and when Milton says at the opening of Book IX that he must change his 'Notes to Tragic' (6) he makes a calculated and not an idle claim. The Christian and non-Christian theories about the role of fortune in the disposition of the world and in the plot of tragedy are brought face to face in the episode of Book IX. Milton develops an ingenious logical exercise on the ideas of choice and chance.

# 6

# The Contention about Knowledge

## I

Other difficulties arise from Genesis. What, for example, did Eve know about the forbidden Tree since her statement to Satan about it was not quite accurate: '3 But of the fruit of the tree which is in the midst of the garden, God hath said, Ye shall not eat of it, neither shall ye touch it, lest ye die' (Genesis 3). But God had said nothing about touching the Tree, and Eve's 'lest ye die' makes the doom sound not utterly inevitable as was often enough pointed out: 'In which delivery there were no less than two mistakes, or rather additional mendacities; for the Commandment forbad not the touch of the Fruit; and positively, said, Ye shall surely die.'[1] But why should Eve be misinformed, or why should she lie? Milton, through the invention of additional dialogue, is careful to show that Eve knows the truth, as we see from Adam's words to her: 'for well thou knowst/God hath pronounc't it death to taste that Tree' (IV, 426-427), and she (unlike the Eve of Genesis) makes no mistake when she is talking with Satan: 'In the day we eate/Of this fair Fruit, our doom is, we shall die' (IX, 762-763). Indeed Milton is so anxious to clear Eve of error that in his managing of the matter he makes one of his own. Since he has necessarily to

[1] Browne, *Vulgar Errors.* (*Works*, II, 18-19).

97

follow Genesis, the idea of touching the Fruit has to appear in her conversation with Satan, as it does when she tells him:

> But of this Tree we may nor taste, nor touch . . .
> (IX, 651)
> But of the Fruit of this fair Tree amidst
> The Garden, God hath said, Ye shall not eate
> Thereof, nor shall ye touch it, least ye die.
> (IX, 661-663)

She is still not in error or lying (as Browne for example supposed) since the correct idea of eating is there. But does the addition of touching matter, or in any way alter the offence? Certainly eating the Fruit when even touching it was forbidden would seem all the more heinous an offence, which is precisely the view that Adam takes when he learns what Eve has done: 'Much more to taste it under banne to touch' (IX, 925). But where did Adam get the idea that there might be a ban on touching as well as on tasting the Tree? Eve has spoken only of tasting, the word occurring six times in her speech to him, the word 'eat'n' once (IX, 869), the word 'touch' not at all. And he cannot know what has passed between Eve and the serpent. But the word 'touch' is at one other place associated with the ban, when Milton is summing up Raphael's injuctions to Adam:

> Say, Goddess, what ensu'd when *Raphael*,
> The affable Arch-Angel, had forewarn'd
> *Adam* by dire example to beware
> Apostasie, by what befell in Heaven
> To those Apostates, least the like befall
> In Paradise to *Adam* or his Race,
> Charg'd not to touch the interdicted Tree,
> If they transgress, and slight that sole command,
> So easily obeyd amid the choice
> Of all tastes else to please thir appetite,
> Though wandring.
> (VII, 40-50)

The difficulty is that they have not been charged not to touch the Tree. It looks from this as though Milton, anxious to insist that 'touch' was no mere mistake of Eve's, had decided that this meant not only getting the certainty of death and the importance of 'taste' across to her, but also getting the idea of touching across to Adam. But the speech that was to do it is not there.

Another difficulty arising out of the Genesis account of Eve's meeting with Satan is that she was obviously deceived about the identity of her tempter. Genesis says nothing whatever about Satan. Milton's first solution to this is to insist that the possibility of Adam and Eve's being deceived is in no way an indictment of God's providence. Adam, talking with Eve before she parts from him (and thus incidentally warning her), emphasizes the deceptiveness of appearances:

> Against his will he can receave no harme.
> But God left free the Will, for what obeyes
> Reason, is free, and Reason he made right,
> But bid her well beware, and still erect,
> Least by some faire appeering good surpris'd
> She dictate false, and misinforme the Will
> To do what God expressly hath forbid.
>
> (IX, 350-356)

and, looking back at the Fall from the opening of Book X, Milton makes the same necessary logical point about their temptation:

> For still they knew, and ought to have still remember'd
> The high Injunction not to taste that Fruit,
> Whoever tempted . . .
>
> (X, 12-14)

No matter to whom they may be talking, God's command not to eat the Fruit still stands.

It was in order to explicate this very important fact that Eve's being deceived was not improvident that Milton invents the episode of Uriel's encounter with Satan earlier in the poem. For Uriel, the angel of the sun, failed also to see that the cherub to whom he was talking was Satan in disguise:

So spake the false dissembler unperceivd;
For neither Man nor Angel can discern
Hypocrisie, the onely evil that walks
Invisible, except to God alone,
By his permissive will, through Heav'n and Earth . . .
(III, 681-685)

The episode makes an attractive little moral fable, but its real function is with regard to the interpretation of the Fall. The phrase 'permissive will' indicates this. To use it of Uriel's encounter with Satan makes rather a lot of it, but Milton is concerned with the more important issue that Satan, again in disguise, was permitted later to tempt Eve. Failure to penetrate a disguise is made an attribute that men share with angels and thus can hardly be supposed an imperfection. The episode serves to exemplify one of the most important tactics in the argument of *Paradise Lost*, the ascribing of certain attributes to angels in order to support the thesis that is being developed about the Fall.[2] Even so Milton may have thought that this inability to see through deceit was a bit hard on angels since Uriel is not fooled for long: when Satan lands on Niphates' top Uriel observes his demonic manner and reports his presence to the angelic guard. The matter makes also for some difficulty in the case of this guard. For if Uriel cannot penetrate Satan's disguise, then neither can the guard, and what is the use of a guard if it cannot distinguish friend from foe? Milton meets this awkwardness by providing the guard with a magic stick which has the power to restore any creature to its proper shape (IV, 810-814). This is perhaps somewhat fanciful, but the point where it all started—Eve's failure to see through Satan's disguise—was too crucial to be ignored.

This particular episode is for the reader's benefit and helps

---

[2] On Milton's angelology, see Robert H. West, *Milton and the Angels*, (Athens, Ga., 1955). My concern is more with the way in which Milton selects certain attributes in order to explicate the Fall.

Eve herself not at all since she does not know about it. Milton's second tactic in the face of the difficulty is to provide extensive warning for Eve about what might happen to her if she is not careful. She is firstly warned about the subtle nature of the serpent. The first scene in the Garden

> close the Serpent sly
> Insinuating, wove with Gordian twine
> His breaded train, and of his fatal guile
> Gave proof unheeded . . . (IV, 347-350)

provides, for the benefit of Adam and Eve, a demonstration of insidiousness, physically exemplified in the serpent's motion. This is reinforced by the deviousness of its progress when it leads Eve to the forbidden Tree: 'rowld/In tangles, and made intricate seem strait' (IX, 631-632). Eve's speech to him when they are there shows that she is not unaware of his subtlety: 'Thee, Serpent, suttlest Beast of all the field/I knew' (IX, 560-561). Milton takes this description of the serpent from the Genesis narrative (3: 1) and makes it part of Eve's speech in order to clear away any imputations that there might be against God's providence on the issue of what Eve knew about the serpent. Secondly Eve is warned about the true nature of her tempter. The episode of her dream shows her tempted not by a snake but by someone who, using all the subtlety of the snake, is in appearance an angel. Eve is there faced with what is to be the truth:

> And as I wondring lookt, beside it stood
> One shap'd and wing'd like one of those from Heav'n
> By us oft seen; his dewie locks distill'd
> Ambrosia . . . (V, 54-57)

The dream is of course inspired by Satan but it is made to serve God's purposes. And thirdly Eve is not ignorant of their enemy and his power. Her conversation with Adam before they separate provides important leads here. Eve has been told by Adam and by Raphael about the danger as she reveals:

That such an Enemie we have, who seeks
Our ruin, both by thee informd I learne,
And from the parting Angel over-heard
As in a shadie nook I stood behind,
Just then returnd at shut of Evening Flours.

(IX, 274-278)

but Adam now builds up a fuller picture for her. He argues
that Satan's success in tempting even angels is proof of his
subtlety: 'Suttle he needs must be, who could seduce/Angels'
(IX, 307-308), and Eve's description of Satan as a 'Foe,/Suttle
or violent' (IX, 323-324) in her next speech shows that she
has taken the point. Finally, in his last speech to her Adam
warns her that she might meet 'Some specious object by the
Foe subornd' (IX, 361). Thus, even if Eve did not see through
the serpent's disguise or subtlety at the actual moment when he
appeared before her in her temptation—and Genesis would
seem to indicate that she did not—Milton has nevertheless
carefully contrived a set of incidents and speeches so as to
leave her in no way unprepared against that situation. The
poem is governed by the logic of its thesis.

II

But Milton has a much more difficult problem with the fall of
Eve, one concerned not with what Genesis does not say but
with what it does. This problem is the nature of the forbidden
Tree:

9 And out of the ground made the LORD God to grow every
tree that is pleasant to the sight and good for food; the tree of
life also in the midst of the garden, and the tree of knowledge of
good and evil.

16 And the LORD God commanded the man, saying, Of every
tree of the garden thou mayest freely eat:

17 But of the tree of the knowledge of good and evil, thou shalt
not eat of it: for in the day that thou eatest thereof thou shalt
surely die.

(Genesis 2)

4 And the serpent said unto the woman, Ye shall not surely die; 5 For God doth know that in the day ye eat thereof, then your eyes shall be opened, and ye shall be as gods, knowing good and evil.
6 And when the woman saw that the tree was good for food, and that it was pleasant to the eyes, and a tree to be desired to make one wise, she took of the fruit thereof, and did eat, and gave also unto her husband with her; and he did eat.
7 And the eyes of them both were opened, and they knew that they were naked;

22 And the LORD God said, Behold, the man is become as one of us to know good and evil.

(Genesis 3)

In the heavenly dimension of the poem the nature of the Tree is not relevant. The injunction not to eat of its Fruit is simply a test of Man's obedience, and the plot of *Paradise Lost* on this level includes no details of the Tree. In Book III, 80-134 when God sets forth the principles on which his world is governed, and in Book V, 224-245 when he despatches Raphael to Earth in order to reinforce Adam and Eve's sense of their obligation to the command, he talks only of obedience, not of the Tree. But in the earthly dimension of the poem the matter was necessarily more involved, and this was where the details of the Genesis account became important and sometimes puzzling. What Genesis says about the Tree is this. Its Fruit is pleasant to see and to taste, but, once eaten, it effects a change in the nature of the creature that eats it, making those who eat it like gods by conferring upon them a special sort of knowledge, the knowledge of good and evil, that belongs to gods. The account also seems to imply that this knowledge was the same as knowing oneself (or Man) to be naked. This is the material that *Paradise Lost* builds into a very elaborate yet very logical system that supports its central thesis about God's providence.

The first problem is one about knowledge. The Tree clearly has something to do with this: there is its name and Eve's perception that it was a Tree to be desired to make one wise.

It would be absurd to suppose that its name ('the tree of the knowledge of good and evil') meant that Man before the Fall had no knowledge of the good, this coming to him only with the eating of the forbidden Tree. So Milton makes Adam and Eve in their innocent state perfectly aware of the good, provided and real, which they enjoy: their hymns of praise at evening (IV, 724-735) and morning (V, 153-208) acknowledge their blessings and their Maker's bounty. And they know too that it would be evil to eat of the forbidden Tree and to disobey. So Milton adopts the conventional gloss that the knowledge of good and evil means the knowledge of good lost and evil got, as Adam's speech after the Fall indicates:

> and find we know
> Both Good and Evil, Good lost and Evil got,
> Bad Fruit of Knowledge, if this be to know . . .
> (IX, 1071-1073)

a sort of knowledge which was, before the Fall, properly and providentially forbidden.

But Eve's recognition that the Tree was 'to be desired to make one wise' makes no qualification about what particular sort of knowledge the Tree conferred, and Milton (conventionally) more usually calls the Tree simply the Tree of Knowledge. If it is so called, then it follows from what Genesis says that there is a sort of knowledge which God and the angels have but which is forbidden to men. And although in Genesis the question of knowledge is raised in the temptation of Eve, the real interest of the case lies in relation to Adam. It means that God has denied him some sort of knowledge, and this limitation, given the theme of the poem, has to be shown to be reasonable and compatible with God's providence. That it is not so is precisely the line that Satan adopts when he hears of it:

> Knowledge forbidd'n?
> Suspicious, reasonless. Why should thir Lord
> Envie them that? can it be sin to know,
> Can it be death? and do they onely stand

> By Ignorance, is that thir happie state,
> The proof of thir obedience and thir faith?
>
> (IV, 515-520)

His decision that he will tempt them to intemperance in knowledge

> Hence I will excite thir minds
> With more desire to know, and to reject
> Envious commands, invented with designe
> To keep them low whom knowledge might exalt
> Equal with Gods; aspiring to be such,
> They taste and die . . .
>
> (IV, 522-527)

usefully combines the two things that Genesis says about the Tree: the desire to eat the Fruit in order to become wise is linked with its power to make the eater like the gods. In this way the matter—and in particular Eve's motives—can be given a moral gloss, showing intemperance (*more* desire to know) and pride (to be like the gods).

This tactic served easily enough to explicate the moral issue at the Fall, where the important question is not what knowledge is about but with what feelings and motives it is pursued. Satan, tempting Eve, emphasizes the connection of the Fruit with enlightenment:

> O Sacred, Wise and Wisdom-giving Plant,
> Mother of Science, Now I feel thy Power
> Within mee cleere, not only to discerne
> Things in thir Causes, but to trace the wayes
> Of highest Agents, deemd however wise.
>
> (IX, 679-683)

thus including in his temptation the Genesis material of becoming wise and like the gods, but he is only pretending to have knowledge (his speech is false and senseless) in order to incite Eve to desire more than she ought. So when Eve, desiring to be wise, experiences 'expectation high/Of knowledg, nor was God-head from her thought' (IX, 789-790) and when Adam in his turn calls the Fruit's power of making those who eat it like the gods an 'inducement strong' (IX, 934), the Fall is read in terms of the moral issue of pride. Knowledge has nothing to do with the matter at all, and the only knowledge that Adam and Eve acquire as the result of their act is ironical, the knowledge of the 'Good lost, and Evil got' (IX, 1072). The account in Book IX, properly presenting the episode in a moral way, does not deal with the question of what the forbidden knowledge is.

This question was important.[3] Knowledge was a vital and providential weapon in the war against distress and sin, yet the apparent limit on knowledge which Genesis imposed had, since Genesis spoke with the best authority in the world, to be made reasonable. Bacon for example had to outline his position very cautiously with regard to this problem: Genesis could become a dangerous weapon in the hands of the pious obscurantist, just as science could in the hands of the impious rationalist:

> I hear the former sort say, that knowledge is of those things which are to be accepted of with great limitation and caution; that the aspiring to overmuch knowledge was the original temptation and sin, whereupon ensu'd the fall of man; that knowledge hath in it something of the serpent, and therefore where it entereth into a man it makes him swell . . .
>
> To discover then the ignorance and error of this opinion, and the misunderstanding in the grounds therof, it may well appear these men do not observe or consider that it was not the pure knowledge of nature and universality, a knowledge by the light whereof man did give names unto other creatures in Paradise, as they were brought before him, according unto their proprieties, which gave the occasion to the fall; but it was the proud knowledge of good and evil, with an intent in man to give law unto himself and to depend no more upon God's commandments, which was the form of the temptation.[4]

---

[3] For the whole question see Schultz, *Milton and Forbidden Knowledge*. My own approach is much narrower, being concerned with the logical 'fit' with Genesis.

[4] *Advancement of Learning*, Book I. (*Works*, ed. Spedding (London, 1857), III, 264-265).

Bacon, anxious to establish some contact with the idea of a forbidden knowledge, argues by a series of discriminations. His first is based on amount: it is 'overmuch knowledge' that is wrong. His second is between the right and wrong ways of acquiring knowledge, the wrong way being followed through pride ('makes him swell,' 'the proud knowledge of good and evil'). On this reading motive is important and so Bacon, like Milton, is enabled to put the matter usefully on to a moral level. It is interesting to see how Bacon, in his contrast between the 'pure knowledge of nature and universality' and the 'proud knowledge of good and evil' (my italics), smuggles a moral distinction into what is basically a distinction between types of knowledge.

This question of knowledge was a vital one because the history of Man, even when seen as the history of God's purposes, included the growth of reason in insight and application. Man before the Fall was after all not merely virtuous. He was also comfortable, catching no colds, suffering no migraine. From this point of view aspirin as well as moral integrity will win back man's happy state. Bacon's last Aphorism thus links the new science with the old Biblical injunction to Man to rule over nature: 'Only let the human race recover that right over nature which belongs to it by divine bequest, and let power be given it; the exercise thereof will be governed by sound reason and true religion.'[5] To such projects for advancement, education and the growth of knowledge are crucial. Johnson too saw history as the history of human rationality and of progress in understanding and manipulation. His Journey to the Western Islands of Scotland ends most touchingly with the account of Mr Braidwood who had discovered a technique by which the deaf might be taught: 'It was pleasing to see one of the most desperate of human calamities capable of so much help: whatever enlarges hope, will exalt courage; after having seen the deaf taught

---

[5] Aphorisms concerning the Interpretation of Nature etc., No. CXXIX. (Works, IV, 115).

arithmetick, who would be afraid to cultivate the *Hebrides?*[6] Milton also saw knowledge as a precious human gift. *Of Education* looks especially to this remedial aspect of knowledge and asserts (with characteristic boldness) that knowledge, operant after the Fall, is the salvation and not the corruption of man: 'The end then of Learning is to repair the ruines of our first Parents' (IV, 277). So too in *Paradise Lost* God's providence after the Fall extends not only to a reassuring vision of Christian history, but also to the instructing of Adam in technical skills. God provides him with clothes made from skins; Adam finds the use of fire (Book X). Knowledge is remedial and useful and enables Man after the Fall to pass his life commodiously.

## III

Milton, like many other commentators, insists from the start on a learned and contemplative Adam. His unfallen Adam has knowledge of his own nature and its needs, and also a knowledge of universal nature, shown in his naming of the animals as they were brought before him, the naming being taken to involve the knowledge of them:

> I nam'd them, as they pass'd, and understood
> Thir Nature, with such knowledg God endu'd
> My sudden apprehension . . .
>
> (VIII, 352-354)

Milton's Eve is also made to share much of Adam's knowledge. Although at the opening of Book VIII she leaves the company when she sees that Adam is entering upon 'studious thoughts abstruse' (VIII, 40), Milton makes it clear that she does this not because she is not interested in abstruse things but because she preferred, quite properly, to hear about them from her husband. Milton thus goes out of his way to show that Eve is capable of 'what was high' (VIII, 50). The thesis of the forbidden knowledge does not imply an unintellectual human pair.

[6] Ed. R. W. Chapman (Oxford, 1924), p. 148.

But Milton still has to give some body to that thesis. The poem first comes to grips with the issue in the encounter between Uriel and Satan which, besides being used to make a point about deceit, also serves to spell out a homily upon knowledge. Disguised as a stripling cherub Satan tells Uriel that his desire in coming to the earth is a desire for more knowledge:

> Unspeakable desire to see, and know
> All these his wondrous works, but chiefly Man . . .
> (III, 662-663)

Satan keeps up his cherubic disguise very cleverly, for his desire to know is directed to the proper end since it ends in the knowledge of the glory of God:

> That both in him and all things, as is meet,
> The Univeral Maker we may praise . . .
> (III, 675-676)

This earns him a compliment from Uriel:

> Faire Angel, thy desire which tends to know
> The works of God, thereby to glorifie
> The great Work-Maister, leads to no excess
> That reaches blame, but rather merits praise
> The more it seems excess . . .
> (III, 694-698)

Milton, with his eye on Genesis and the desire to be wise, is again using the angels to sound out themes central to the understanding of the Fall. Uriel's point is that the desire for more knowledge of the works of God is not at all excessive or sinful provided it is moved by the right reason, for God's praise and not man's pride. But Milton, as is seen when Uriel describes the works of God that lie before them, has made a careful choice of his scene:

> But what created mind can comprehend
> Thir number, or the wisdom infinite
> That brought them forth, but hid thir causes deep.
> I saw when at his Word the formless Mass,

This worlds material mould, came to a heap:
*Confusion* heard his voice, and wilde uproar
Stood rul'd, stood vast infinitude confin'd;
Till at his second bidding darkness fled,
Light shon, and order from disorder sprung:
Swift to thir several Quarters hasted then
The cumbrous Elements, Earth, Flood, Aire, Fire,
And this Ethereal quintessence of Heav'n
Flew upward, spirited with various forms,
That rowld orbicular, and turnd to Starrs
Numberless, as thou seest, and how they move;
Each had his place appointed, each his course,
The rest in circuit walles this Universe.

(III, 705-721)

Here, in the wide prospect of the sky, is the astronomer's
view. It is a suitable book for the angels to read since they
have wings to fly amongst the starry worlds. But the opening of
Uriel's speech sounds some significant warnings. It is a hard
book to read: God's wisdom, which is not fully to be understood by any of his creatures, has its secrets, its hidden causes.
This is Milton's first glance at the forbidden faces of knowledge.
That God had his secrets was a commonplace for which there
was ample warrant. Some of them were indeed, according to
*The Christian Doctrine*, hidden even from the Son: 'there being
some secret purposes, the knowledge of which the Father has
reserved to himself alone' (XIV, 317-319). The Book of Job 38
gives a brief glimpse into some of them, those of creation and
of the sea. But the full truth about them is known to none. So if
Genesis clearly implies that God and his angels are unlike Man in
respect of their knowledge of certain things, Milton also insists
that the angels are like Man in their ignorance of certain
things. Milton's proceeding by likeness and unlikeness works
helpfully here: God's limitation of Man's knowledge looks less
improvident if it turns out that the angels share some (though
not all) of these limitations too. Some of the secrets of the
Creation were, as Uriel tells Satan, hidden from him (III, 707).

This episode is thus an important prelude to what the poem has to say about knowledge, and it occupies some important positions. It shows what the propriety of knowledge consists of, focuses attention on to the Heavens as the book of God and establishes that God has secrets. Adam's conversation with Raphael continues the debate. Raphael's visit provides the opportunity for those digressions (on the Fall of the Angels, the Creation, etc.) that were an expected part of the epic poem and they convey delight, wonder and awe, but Milton also makes them contribute logically to his thesis about the Fall. They are made to bear upon the question of Man's knowledge. Milton's tactics are especially neat. They are to open and close the various episodes with discussions that are concerned with the specific issue of knowledge, thus keeping alive the whole time the important question of curiosity, providing extensively for its gratification, and yet also looking always to the idea of there being a limit.

First he is careful to insist that true knowledge begins and ends with God. Raphael's scale of nature speech instructs Adam about the way in which the universe depends upon its Maker:

> O *Adam*, one Almightie is, from whom
> All things proceed, and up to him return . . .
>
> (V, 469-470)

Here is what Bacon called 'the pure knowledge of nature and universality' laid open and read in the light of God's power and munificence. This natural theology is a suitable subject for an unfallen Adam to concern himself with. But it is a deductive subject and all knowledge clearly cannot be of that order: the idea that there was a forbidden knowledge would be nonsense if all things were open to deduction. In the light of this Milton also marks another unlikeness between angels and men when Raphael points out that angelic knowledge is most often intuitive, human knowledge most often discursive (V, 488-489), for again if human knowledge was intuitive there would be no point in God's imposing a limit upon it.[7] God's forbidding Adam some knowledge must mean that Adam can come at some truths only by instruction or investigation. So secondly Milton develops Adam's dialogue with Raphael into a discourse about those matters that were not deductive, and his tactic is to widen the range of Adam's knowledge as much as possible. Recognizing that God had forbidden some knowledge to Adam, he proceeds to show how little God had really denied him.

Adam's first cautious sounding is about angelic digestion: he is not sure that Raphael can eat their dinner

> unsavourie food perhaps
> To spiritual Natures; only this I know,
> That one Celestial Father gives to all.
>
> (V, 401-403)

Adam's awareness that God provides for all is very creditable, but he needs to move carefully over the question of what angels eat. This might, in the light of Genesis, be a dangerous query since it is concerned with the difference between angels (gods) and men, something very relevant to the Fall. Nor is the question in any way to Adam a deductive one since he is talking to a real enough angel. Raphael does not deny him the knowledge but instructs Adam about angelic food, so after their meal Adam pushes a bit more with his desire

> to know
> Of things above his World, and of thir being
> Who dwell in Heav'n . . .
>
> (V, 454-456)

[7] Hoopes, *Right Reason in the Renaissance*, pp. 197-199 sees Milton as recommending intuitive reasoning as best for Man, and discursive reasoning (identified with science) as wrong. Satan is thus seen as the apostle of the discursive reason, and the devils' debate is an exercise in it. I think that this view draws the wrong conclusion from Raphael's differentiation between Man and Angel since, if intuitive reason is best for Man, this seems to recommend that Man should try (if one can try about this) to make himself as much like an angel as possible. (A view identical with Empson's (*Milton's God*, pp. 154-159) though the latter is more concerned with flying than knowing and points out that Eve's reliance on her intuition, typically feminine on the modern view, is also typically angelic on Milton's view.)

Milton calls this request of Adam's a 'wary speech' (V, 459) and it is easy to see why. The delicate question of knowledge is being deliberately raised, and since Adam's request is concerned with the skies and angels, he may well, for all that he knows, be asking for that knowledge which is known to angels but forbidden to men. This turns out not to be the case for Raphael discourses extensively to him about the nature of angels. But this discourse itself, containing as it does the information that some in Heaven have been found disobedient, serves to excite Adam's curiosity as to how heavenly beings could thus fail in virtue. This curiosity Raphael also consents to satisfy but adds a significant warning to his consent since the matter will involve his unfolding 'The secrets of another world, perhaps/Not lawful to reveal' (V, 569-570). It may, since it is about angels, be beyond Man's capacity or forbidden. However this knowledge in its turn is not withheld because it is useful. Raphael's commission, as the argument to Book V shows, was to admonish Man about his obedience, to inform him of his danger and '*whatever else may avail* Adam *to know*.' This passport to knowledge manifests God's providence in its remedial role. The celestial history in which Adam is instructed is, like all good history, exemplary: it teaches 'By terrible example' (VI, 910) what happens to those who because of their disobedience are justly subject to God's anger. But if the history of Heaven is thus permissible and instructive, then so might be the history of Earth before Adam himself was created, something again known to God and angels but not to Adam:

> and now
> Led on, yet sinless, with desire to know
> What neerer might concern him, how this World
> Of Heav'n and Earth conspicuous first began,
> When, and whereof created, for what cause,
> What within *Eden* or without was done
> Before his memorie . . .
> (VII, 60-66)

Milton's juxtaposition here of 'yet sinless' and 'desire to know' shows him still on the same careful course. Adam, though his curiosity is made explicitly not sinful, treads very circumspectly. He justifies his request for more knowledge by its usefulness ('What may no less perhaps availe us known' (VII, 85), and by the fact that his motive is not curiosity about God's secrets but the praise of God:

> if unforbid thou maist unfould
> What wee, not to explore the secrets aske
> Of his Eternal Empire, but the more
> To magnifie his works, the more we know.
>
> (VII, 94-97)

Raphael, again granting his request, notes Adam's proper caution and adds his own important warning:

> This also thy request with caution askt
> Obtaine: though to recount Almightie works
> What words or tongue of Seraph can suffice,
> Or heart of man suffice to comprehend?
> Yet what thou canst attain, which best may serve
> To glorifie the Maker, and inferr
> Thee also happier, shall not be withheld
> Thy hearing, such Commission from above
> I have receav'd, to answer thy desire
> Of knowledge within bounds; beyond abstain
> To ask, nor let thine own inventions hope
> Things not reveal'd, which th'invisible King,
> Onely Omniscient, hath supprest in Night,
> To none communicable in Earth or Heaven:
> Anough is left besides to search and know.
> But Knowledge is as food, and needs no less
> Her Temperance over Appetite, to know
> In measure what the mind may well contain,
> Oppresses else with Surfet, and soon turns
> Wisdom to Folly, as Nourishment to Winde.
>
> (VII, 111-130)

Raphael is concerned with two things here. Firstly, by uttering a warning about intemperance in knowledge, he is outlining the moral approach to the issue that, as discussed earlier in this chapter, becomes relevant in Book IX. Secondly, he warns Adam about the wrong sort of knowledge, the knowledge of God's secrets known neither to Angel nor Man. But, that warning given, he then recounts to Adam the story of the six days of Creation, a story of munificence and power. The solemnity of his warning has thus in no way debarred him from providing Adam with the knowledge for which he had asked. It is essential to see what Milton is doing. If we ignore what Genesis says and implies about this issue of knowledge, then it can look as though he is being surlily obscurantist, meanly and with an ill grace providing Adam with his ration of knowledge. But rather, insisting that he is all the time on course, mindful always of the fact that something is forbidden, Milton moves further and further in the liberation of the mind. Accepting the limitation because he must, he makes of it as little as he can. And he is always concerned to discuss those things which might seem more properly to belong to angels and not to men, to questions of celestial nature and history. He was provided with a nice exercise in the drawing up of a justified though apparently dangerous curriculum. Genesis logically compelled him to set up a system of warnings and reservations, but his thesis about God's providence and his own concern for knowledge as a vital human distinction and privilege insisted that he provide extensively for Adam's instruction.

IV

But although he has been busy indicating all those things that the forbidden knowledge is not, Milton has not yet defined what it is. So in Book VIII he identifies his intellectual scapegoat and, as Satan's encounter with Uriel earlier in the poem had hinted, it turns out to be astronomy. Raphael begins the discussion by asking Adam if there is anything further that he would like to know, making his usual reservation about a limit: 'If else thou seekst/Aught, not surpassing human measure, say' (VII, 639–640). Adam enters badly upon the business by telling Raphael that he marvels that the universe should be made so disproportionately in that the purpose of the myriad moving stars is to give light to the single sedentary Earth:

> reasoning I oft admire,
> How Nature wise and frugal could commit
> Such disproportions, with superfluous hand
> So many nobler bodies to create . . .
>
> (VIII, 24–27)

Such speculations, coming dangerously close to indicting God's providence, show the student of the sky arguing badly about final causes. This apparent failure of judgment does not of course make Adam a fallen creature: it is not approved or indulged. Raphael, playing his proper admonitory role, goes on to deduce a different case from the facts:

> And for the Heav'ns wide Circuit, let it speak
> The Makers high magnificence, who built
> So spacious, and his Line stretcht out so farr;
> That Man may know he dwells not on his own;
> An Edifice too large for him to fill,
> Lodg'd in a small partition, and the rest
> Ordain'd for uses to his Lord best known.
>
> (VIII, 100–106)

These arguments about final causes all imply God's providence and wisdom. On the assumption that the Earth is the still centre of the universe this is what right reasoning about final causes will look like. That this seems to confirm the uselessness of arguments about final causes, in that they can be developed whether the details of the case are true or false, is irrelevant to Milton's purpose. If Adam did think that the Earth was the centre of the universe (as he did), then, in a poem whose subject is God's providence, Milton has to insist that when final causes are looked to, they are looked to in the right way. Milton of course makes a good point about Adam's intelligence in that this idea that it might be more convenient if the Earth itself were to move brings him close to the truth. Raphael continues the discussion by going on to put as a supposition what he himself knows to be the true case:

> What if the Sun
> Be Center to the World, and other Starrs
> By his attractive vertue and thir own
> Incited, dance about him various rounds?
> (VIII, 122-125)

and he allies this with other suggestions, carefully left vague, about life on other worlds. His point is that these are matters best left alone:

> Sollicit not thy thoughts with matters hid,
> Leave them to God above, him serve and feare;
> Of other Creatures, as him pleases best,
> Wherever plac't, let him dispose: joy thou
> In what he gives to thee, this Paradise
> And thy fair *Eve*; Heav'n is for thee too high
> To know what passes there; be lowlie wise:
> Think onely what concernes thee and thy being;
> Dream not of other Worlds, what Creatures there
> Live, in what state, condition, or degree,
> Contented that thus farr hath been reveal'd
> Not of Earth onely but of highest Heav'n.
> (VIII, 167-178)

Milton has at last given some substance to the idea of a forbidden knowledge. It is a knowledge of the sky and other worlds. The matter no doubt had much contemporary interest, but Milton is not really adding to a topical debate.[8] His case is throughout looking to Genesis, so astronomy was a

---

[8] For this debate, see Grant McColley, *Paradise Lost: an Account of its Growth and Major Origins* (Chigago, 1940), pp. 217-244.

logical subject to choose. If the forbidden knowledge belongs to angels and not to men, then the study of the sky can be related to the different natures and capacities of men and angels since angels can fly there and men cannot. So Raphael's exhortation to Adam to be 'lowlie wise' is not essentially a recommendation to intellectual humility. The wisdom that properly belongs to Man is lowly because Man, having no wings, cannot get himself off the ground. It might be supposed that in one respect, the invention of the telescope, man had equipped himself to share something of the vision of angels. It is his sense of this in relation to his own thesis that makes Milton point out earlier in the poem that Man even with the telescope has not the assured clearsightedness of Raphael the angel:

> From hence, no cloud, or, to obstruct his sight,
> Starr interpos'd, however small he sees,
> Not unconform to other shining Globes,
> Earth, and the Gard'n of God, with Cedars crownd
> Above all Hills. As when by night the Glass
> Of *Galileo*, less assur'd, observes
> Imagind Lands and Regions in the Moon . . .
>
> (V, 257-263)

Milton admired Galileo on many counts, but he plays down the scope of the telescope here in comparison with the scope of angels' eyes (Galileo's Glass being less assured than Raphael's sight) in order to forward his own case about the knowledge not proper to Man.

The choice of astronomy had other advantages. Given what Genesis says, the forbidden knowledge has to be something that God and the angels know but that Adam does not, but it would be most helpful if it turned out also to be something that Milton and his readers know but that Adam did not. The fact unknown to Adam can be seen to be a fact. And it was not unreasonable to suppose that Adam did think that the sun went round the Earth. The latter is, according to Genesis, created first and seems in Genesis to be at the centre of things. (Milton himself naturally follows the Genesis sequence of creation in his own account of the Creation in Book VII, but he deliberately does not commit himself to any particular cosmology at that point.) And the story of Joshua's bidding the sun to stand still (Joshua 10: 12), which clearly indicates an Old Testament belief in a geocentric universe and which proved a potent weapon in the hands of the clerical opponents of the new astronomy, could easily give a useful lead on Adam's case. In accomodating himself and his ways to human understanding God had obviously in the Scriptures been content to present a geocentric system. That the heliocentric system was thus not known to the Adam of Genesis gives Milton's example some point.

Furthermore the fact that there was still controversy over these issues among his contemporaries also made his choice of subject a good one. There was dispute as to whether other worlds were or were not inhabited. Milton's own comic Limbo farcically contributes to the debate, Milton solemnly asserting that the likeliest inhabitants of the moon are beings in whose existence he did not believe:

> Not in the neighbouring Moon, as some have dreamd;
> Those argent Fields more likely habitants,
> Translated Saints, or middle Spirits hold
> Betwixt th'Angelical and Human kinde . . .
> (III, 459-462)

The problem of the structure of the universe was also not one of simple alternatives. Raphael points out that even if the sun is the centre of the system, then there is more than one possible way of arrangement:

> or if they list to try
> Conjecture, he his Fabric of the Heav'ns
> Hath left to thir disputes, perhaps to move
> His laughter at thir quaint Opinions wide
> Hereafter, when they come to model Heav'n

And calculate the Starrs, how they will weild
The mightie frame, how build, unbuild, contrive
To save appeerances, how gird the Sphear
With Centric and Eccentric scribl'd o're,
Cycle and Epicycle, Orb in Orb . . .

(VIII, 75-84)

Taking the lead from St Paul's strictures on the wisdom of
the world whose disputers God has made foolish (I Corinthians
1: 20), Milton makes the controversies of astronomy enough
to make God laugh. This absurd note (stuck also in Raphael's
jesting argument about final causes: God's purpose is his own
amusement) is very important. Scepticism is made to look
sensible so that we are led to look on the forbidden knowledge
as something reasonably forbidden. The presence of controversy, the difficulty of verification, the apparent uselessness
of the subject, all contribute to make this study of the sky
sound like speculation rather than knowledge. Milton's position
here is very like that adopted by Arnold in his controversy
with Bishop Colenso where, in religious matters, an edifying
falsehood is seen as preferable to an unedifying truth:

> As speculative opinions about God, theology requires only
> such as are indispensable to the reality of this obedience; the
> belief that God is, that he is a rewarder of them that seek him,
> and that the proof of seeking him is a good life . . . Nay, beyond
> these fundamentals, speculative opinions are pious or impious,
> not as they are true or false, but as they confirm or shake the
> believer in the practice of obedience. The truest speculative
> opinion about the nature of God is impious if it makes its holder
> rebellious; the falsest speculative opinion is pious if it makes him
> obedient.[9]

It is obvious too that Milton is playing the matter very cleverly.
Having defined what the matter of the forbidden knowledge is,
he has diverted the discourse on to the question of what

[9] *Spinoza and the Bible* (*Lectures and Essays in Criticism*, ed. R. H. Super (Ann Arbor,
1962), p. 167).

reasonable purpose it could possibly serve, and Adam's reply
to Raphael, ending this particular debate, underlines this
doctrine of use:

> How fully hast thou satisfi'd mee, pure
> Intelligence of Heav'n, Angel serene,
> And freed from intricacies, taught to live,
> The easiest way, nor with perlexing thoughts
> To interrupt the sweet of Life, from which
> God hath bid dwell farr off all anxious cares,
> And not molest us, unless we our selves
> Seek them with wandring thoughts, and notions vain.
> But apt the Mind or Fancie is to roave
> Uncheckt, and of her roaving is no end;
> Till warn'd, or by experience taught, she learne
> That not to know at large of things remote
> From use, obscure and suttle, but to know
> That which before us lies in daily life,
> Is the prime Wisdom, what is more, is fume,
> Or emptiness, or fond impertinence,
> And renders us in things that most concerne
> Unpractis'd, unprepar'd, and still to seek.
>
> (VIII, 180-197)

Adam's mode of address to Raphael ('pure/Intelligence of
Heav'n') shows the constraints under which the debate has
moved. It marks Adam's acknowledgement of the crucial
distinction between Man and Angel. The forbidden knowledge
is thus about things remote to Man but not to angels who can
fly, and Man's true wisdom is about that world which, since he
is already in it, he has no need to fly to. God is forbidding Man
that sort of knowledge which turns out to be (for him) un-
certain, fruitless, and which does not forward human happiness.
This sounds rational and provident. The particular sort of
knowledge that was involved, the knowledge of the sky, was
an ingenious logical development out of Genesis, but Milton
was more concerned to emphasize the uses of knowledge than
the nature of the one particular kind. His choice of that kind

was tactical because it dealt with worlds the knowledge of which was best achieved by flight and so could be squared with Genesis.[10] He did not by any means always regard astronomy as the forbidden thing. The *Third Prolusion*, attacking the scholastic philosophy (XIII, 169) and *Of Education* (IV, 283) both included astronomy in their recommended subjects. *The Christian Doctrine*, treating the subject with some reservation (largely no doubt because of its connection with astrology, a sometimes more impudent art that did pry into secrets), nevertheless eventually admits it: 'All study of the heavenly bodies, however, is not unlawful or unprofitable; as appears from the journey of the wise men, and still more from the star itself, divinely appointed to announce the birth of Christ, Matt. ii. I, 2' (XVII, 151). Just as, because of what Genesis says, Milton excludes astronomy in Book VIII of *Paradise Lost*, so, because of what St Matthew says, he admits it in *The Christine Doctrine*. His argument in both cases is characteristically apologetic.

The return that Milton makes to the issue at the end of the poem shows the difficulty, perhaps embarrassment, that it has caused him. Since knowledge is so important a gift to man, Adam is made to leave the Garden, not in ignorance but instead with the enlightenment about the future that Michael's visit has given him. He tells Michael that what he has chiefly learned is that 'to obey is best,/And love with fear the onely God' (XII, 557-558). The main stress falls on the moral issues of disobedience and pride, the sins of Book IX. But Michael's reply widens the matter to include the intellectual as well as the moral question:

> To whom thus also th'Angel last repli'd:
> This having learnt, thou hast attaind the summe
> Of wisedom; hope no higher, though all the Starrs

[10] Most critics agree that Milton is not simply adopting an anti-intellectual or anti-scientific attitude (see especially: Schultz, *Milton and Forbidden Knowledge*, pp. 173-183; and Svendsen, *Milton and Science*, p. 78. But for the opposite view, see Arthur O. Lovejoy, 'Milton's Dialogue on Astronomy', *Reason and the Imagination*, ed. J. A. Mazzeo (New York and London, 1962), pp. 129-142.

Thou knewst by name, and all th'ethereal Powers,
All secrets of the deep, all Natures works,
Or works of God in Heav'n, Aire, Earth, or Sea,
And all the riches of this World enjoydst,
And all the rule, one Empire; onely add
Deeds to thy knowledge answerable, add Faith,
Add vertue, Patience, Temperance, add Love,
By name to come call'd Charitie, the soul
Of all the rest: then wilt thou not be loath
To leave this Paradise, but shalt possess
A paradise within thee, happier farr.

(XII, 574-587)

This comes back to the proper provinces of human knowledge.
But since it concerned with Adam after and not before the
Fall, the knowledge of the stars which before the Fall was
given a unique role in the intellectual sphere is now merely
one branch of the knowledge of universal nature, though it is
mentioned first because of its importance earlier in the poem.
And this universal knowledge is sought in order to further the
dominion over nature that had been ordained for Adam at his
creation ('all the rule, one Empire'). Michael, it can be seen,
forbids none of these things. He merely insists on Adam's
knowledge being accompanied with deeds and charity, saying
that, from God's point of view, if Adam is going to be clever,
then he must also ensure that he is good. Milton, deliberately
raising the issue at the close, refuses to abandon his belief in
knowledge as beneficial and remedial. No knowledge, it
turns out, is now forbidden to Man, though some branches of
knowledge are more important than others. Milton's point is
the same as that of the man of learning in *Rasselas*, ch. XL: 'To
man is permitted the contemplation of the skies, but the
practice of virtue is commanded.'

# 7

# The Provocative Fruit

THE second difficulty that the forbidden Tree of Genesis provides is found in the phrase '6 And when the woman saw that the tree was good for food, and that it was pleasant to the eyes' (Genesis 3). Explications of the text were concerned to expand this into a sensible process. It was obviously necessary to insist that Eve was corrupted by her own desire and not by the Tree, for to suppose that the Tree was evil would be to tax God with being the creator of evil. The Fruit was not hurtful, merely forbidden: 'For God would not have planted any hurtful thing in that delicious Paradise. But upon this precept was grounded obedience, the mother and guardian of all the other virtues of the soul: to which it is good to be subject, and pernicious to leave (leaving with it the Creator's will) and to follow one's own.'[1] God's injunction to Man not to eat the Fruit was simply a test of obedience and not a warning made in order to save Man from becoming the victim of some poisonous object. The prohibition was intended to show that the aim of the rational soul lies in subjection to God. It needed no further justification. Calvin follows Augustine on this issue: 'Justly does Augustine complain that God is

[1] Augustine, *City of God* (Book XIV, ch. xii), trans. J. Healy, Dent's Temple Classics (London, 1905), Part III, p. 29.

insulted whenever any higher reason than his will is de-
manded'[2] and argues, specifically about the forbidden Fruit:
'Very dangerous is the temptation, when it is suggested to us,
that God is not to be obeyed, except so far as the reason of his
command is apparent.'[3] This is the point that Milton makes
when Raphael tells Adam about the missions upon which
angels are from time to time sent by God:

> But us he sends upon his high behests
> For state, as Sovran King, and to enure
> Our prompt obedience.
> (VIII, 238-240)

That there seems to be no point in such errands is precisely the
point of them. The episode is another contribution to the set of
likenesses between Man and Angel that is developed in the
poem. Angels too have to obey even if the reason of what they
are commanded is not known to them.

The difficulty is that Genesis presents a Tree that is not merely
forbidden but also attractive in aspect and taste, and it was
necessary to insist that God had not made the forbidden Fruit
provocative, thus almost inciting Man to sin. That Milton had
himself in *Areopagitica* described it as provocative must not be
allowed to influence the way in which *Paradise Lost* needs to be
read since Milton's argument in *Areopagitica* is not as innocent
as it appears: 'God therefore left him free, set before him a
provoking object, ever almost in his eyes; herein consisted his
merit, herein the right of his reward, the praise of his abstinence'
(IV, 319). The Biblical reference here is tactical and well
suited to Milton's purpose. Putting a case against censorship
Milton finds it helpful to show that God himself saw nothing
untoward in allowing freedom in the midst of provocation:
even if some books are provocative, Biblical precedent provides
a reason for not banning them. But Milton cannot allow the
provocative Fruit into *Paradise Lost*. Skilled in logic, he handles
this particular matter much more intelligently than other

[2] *Institutes* (Book 1, ch. xiv), trans. H. Beveridge, I, 142.
[3] *Commentaries upon Genesis*, trans. J. King (Edinburgh, 1845), I, 147-148.

poets who wrote about the Fall. *Genesis B* for example makes the forbidden Tree of a black, funereal hue, an emblem of the death that the eating of it brings.[4] But besides not tallying with what Genesis says, this makes God go too much out of his way in order to deter Man, and makes Man all the stupider when he is not deterred. Grotius provides a more touching invention. When his Eve comes to pluck the Fruit, it is reluctant, clinging delayingly to its bough.[5] But this is a mistake too. The Fruit itself must be indifferent. It will neither help nor hinder. It is neither compliant nor reluctant, neither grim nor provocative. Any intelligent reading of the matter must make the sinful act and the responsibility for it Man's alone. The temptation of the senses, as the best commentators saw, must follow the temptation of the heart.

Milton's presentation of the Tree is ingenious. In the heavenly dimension of the poem it is not mentioned at all, God being concerned only with the question of obedience and not with the arrangements by which it was to be tried. In the earthly dimension of the poem, in the Garden, a very simple but effective method is adopted. The crucial phase in Genesis is 'good for food, and pleasant to the eyes.' This is used with reference to all the trees in the Garden when they are first created: '9 And out of the ground made the LORD God to grow every tree that is pleasant to the sight, and good for food; the tree of life also in the midst of the garden, and the tree of knowledge of good and evil' (Genesis 2), and of the forbidden Tree when Eve is tempted: '6 And when the woman saw that the tree was good for food, and that it was pleasant to the eyes . . . she took of the fruit thereof, and did eat' (Genesis 3). Milton needs to establish the point that the forbidden Tree is not in any way provocative. He does this firstly by insisting that all the other unforbidden trees are very provocative indeed. Their beauty is extravagantly stressed:

[4] I. 477.
[5] *Adamus Exul*, Act IV, l. 1267. (See Kirkconnell, *The Celestial Cycle*, p. 170.) Grotius is doubtless imitating *Aeneid*, VI, 211.

Thus was this place,
A happy rural seat of various view;
Groves whose rich Trees wept odorous Gumms and Balme,
Others whose fruit burnisht with Golden Rinde
Hung amiable, *Hesperian* Fables true,
If true, here only, and of delicious taste . . .

(IV, 246-251)

and they are tempting to the appetite, as Adam's account of his dream shows:

Each Tree
Load'n with fairest Fruit that hung to the Eye
Tempting, stirr'd in me sudden appetite
To pluck and eate; whereat I wak'd, and found
Before mine Eyes all real, as the dream
Had lively shadowd . . .

(VIII, 306-311)

The phrase 'pleasant to the sight and good for food' is thus taken very intensively when Milton describes the unforbidden trees of the Garden. But secondly, in contrast to this, he never mentions the beauty of the Tree of Knowledge at all. It first appears in the description of the Garden in Book IV:

in this pleasant soile
His farr more pleasant Garden God ordaind;
Out of the fertil ground he caus'd to grow
All Trees of noblest kind for sight, smell, taste;
And all amid them stood the Tree of Life,
High eminent, blooming Ambrosial Fruit
Of vegetable Gold; and next to Life
Our Death the Tree of knowledge stood fast by,
Knowledge of Good bought dear by knowing ill.

(IV, 214-222)

Here the unnamed trees are beautiful, and the Tree of Life is described with an exotic luxuriance, but the Tree of Knowledge is presented quite flatly. It is not said to be even fair. The same extravagance about one set of trees and the same restraint about the forbidden one is also marked in Adam's account of the trees of the Garden to Eve:

of all the Trees
In Paradise that bear delicious fruit
So various, not to taste that onely Tree
Of knowledge, planted by the Tree of Life,
So neer grows Death to Life, what ere Death is,
Som dreadful thing no doubt; for well thou knowst
God hath pronounc't it death to taste that Tree . . .
(IV, 421-427)

and in Raphael's exhortation to Adam:

He brought thee into this delicious Grove,
This Garden, planted with the Trees of God,
Delectable both to behold and taste;
And freely all thir pleasant fruit for food
Gave thee, all sorts are here that all th'Earth yields,
Varietie without end; but of the Tree
Which tasted works knowledge of Good and Evil,
Thou maist not . . .
(VII, 537-544)

So Milton's tactic, describing the beauty of all the trees in the Garden except the forbidden one, rules out the idea of a provocative forbidden Tree.

But he still has to come to terms with the use of the phrase in Genesis at the moment of Eve's fall (Genesis 3: 6), and here Eve's dream gives a very important lead on his reading of the matter. The dream presents a very different forbidden Tree, for Eve sees it thus:

brough me on a sudden to the Tree
Of interdicted Knowledge: fair it seem'd,
Much fairer to my Fancie then by day . . .
(V, 51-53)

The Tree might, since God is good, be expected to be fair although we are never told that it is. But even in the dream Eve recognizes that the beauty of the Tree is unusual, and when the tempting angel holds out its Fruit to her, there is a significant shift of emphasis:

So saying he drew nigh, and to me held,
Even to my mouth of that same fruit held part
Which he had pluckt; the pleasant savourie smell
So quick'nd appetite, that I, methought,
Could not but taste.

(V, 82-86)

This establishes some crucial things. The forbidden Tree now
provokes appetite in the way that all the other trees of the
Garden do. It has the same effect on Eve that the unforbidden
trees had on Adam when he also had his dream of the Garden
whose trees 'stirr'd in me sudden appetite/To pluck and eate'
(VIII, 308-309). But the account of Eve's dream presses even
harder on this question of appetite when it includes the phrase
'Could not but taste.' For Eve says that, looking now at the
forbidden Tree, she was not merely attracted by its Fruit but
also could not refrain from eating it because of the appetite
that it aroused. Appetites are by definition natural necessities,
and Eve in her dream finds the natural necessity totally
compelling. There can be no question at all of her being fallen.[6]
This is merely a dream, used to provide providential warning
to her. It gives Eve (and the reader) a drastically but usefully
simplified account of what eventually was to happen at her fall.
The psychological scheme adopted is simple: appetites are
natural necessites but they can in a rational creature be controlled by judgment, as Raphael in his exhortation points out;
'govern well thy appetite' (VII, 546). Eve's dream shows the
natural necessity uncontrolled by judgment, but Eve is not,
when she has it, fallen because sleep, according to the Aristote-
lian psychology that Milton is using, divests the mind of moral
responsibility: 'And because imaginations remain in the
organs of sense and resemble sensations, animals in their
actions are largely guided by them, some (i.e. the brutes)

---

[6] Diekhoff, *Milton's Paradise Lost*, p. 56 takes the view that the dream does arouse
the desires in Eve that are to lead to her downfall, and Millicent Bell, 'The Fallacy of
the Fall etc.,' *PMLA*, LXVIII, argues that the episode shows that Eve is fallen already.
For the opposite view see also H. V. S. Ogden, 'The Crisis of Paradise Lost Recon-
sidered,' *PQ*, XXXVI (1957), 1-19.

because of the non-existence in them of mind, others (i.e. men) because of the temporary eclipse in them of mind by feeling or disease or sleep.'[7] Eve's dream is an exercise of the fancy and the appetite uninfluenced by judgment.[8]

The manner in which Satan addresses her in the dream is part of this process. Poetry also issues from the fancy and appeals to the feelings, and Satan seeks to attract Eve with the most seductive address:

> Why sleepst thou *Eve*? Now is the pleasant time,
> The cool, the silent, save where silence yields
> To the night-warbling Bird, that now awake
> Tunes sweetest his love-labor'd song; now reignes
> Full Orb'd the Moon, and with more pleasant light
> Shadowie sets off the face of things; in vain,
> If none regard; Heav'n wakes with all his eyes,
> Whom to behold but thee, Natures desire,
> In whose sight all things joy, with ravishment
> Attracted by thy beauty still to gaze.
>
> (V, 38-47)

Milton characteristically writes this speech with great logical deliberation. It is a poetry of beautiful unreason. The stars of night do not shine out of their joy in Eve's beauty and it was in order to show up this irrationality that Milton had arranged for Adam to talk with Eve on the previous evening about precisely why they do shine (IV, 660-675). Satan is speaking the satanic poetry that has charm but no sense. Like the songs of Hell it is, for all its 'ravishment,' 'partial' (II, 552), and as love-poetry it is what Milton, assaulting its earthly counterpart, had earlier in the poem contemptuously characterized as the 'Serenate, which the starv'd Lover sings' (IV, 769).[9] Poetry also needs to be read with judgment.

Milton was clearly aware of the risk that he was taking in

---

[7] *de Anima*, Book III, 3. (Works of Aristotle, trans. W. D. Ross (Oxford, 1931), Vol. III.)

[8] For a fuller account of the psychology involved see Svendsen, *Milton and Science*, pp. 36-38; pp. 181-183.

[9] See Howard Schultz, 'Satan's Serenade,' *PQ*, XXVII (1948), 17-26.

thus making Eve subject to her bad dream, and he is careful to make it have the proper effect on her. That she is upset by it might seem to argue some deficiency in her happiness hardly compatible with life in Paradise, but for her not to be upset by it would be much more disastrous. Her being disturbed shows a reluctance in her to entertain sinful images which is much preferable to her remaining undisturbed by them. So the manner of her sleep during her dream is unusually 'discompos'd' and 'unquiet' (V, 10, 11), and if Milton has brought Eve apparently within a hair's breadth of being a fallen creature, then this also is the way in which it is made most usefully to appear to Eve herself:

> So cheard he his fair Spouse, and she was cheard,
> But silently a gentle tear let fall
> From either eye, and wip'd them with her haire;
> Two other precious drops that ready stood,
> Each in thir Chrystal sluce, hee ere they fell
> Kiss'd as the gracious signs of sweet remorse
> And pious awe, that feard to have offended.
> (V, 129-135)

This illustrates God's providence in its remedial role. For remedy and comfort Eve has her own conscience which is shocked at what she dared even to dream, and the husband with whose solace she is reassured. Adam's comforting address also provides her with a model of the right sort of love song:

> Be not disheart'nd then, nor cloud those looks
> That wont to be more chearful and serene
> Then when fair Morning first smiles on the World,
> And let us to our fresh imployments rise
> Among the Groves, the Fountains, and the Flours
> That open now thir choicest bosom'd smells
> Reserv'd from night, and kept for thee in store.
> (V, 122-128)

Milton has typically developed a nice exercise in a discriminated literary kind. Adam's speech is less extravagent and more sensible than Satan's had been. He talks of them as well as of her, his point that the world is made for their use and pleasure is true and not vain, and he leads Eve into the activities that God had ordained for them and not into sin.

So Milton carefully excludes what would be the wrong implications of Eve's dream. The dream was a useful invention because it enabled Milton to show the decisive role that judgment plays in the moral life. Adam explicates the point for Eve:

> yet be not sad.
> Evil into the mind of God or Man
> May come and go, so unapprov'd, and leave
> No spot or blame behind: Which gives me hope
> That what in sleep thou didst abhorr to dream,
> Waking thou never wilt consent to do.
>
> (V, 116-121)

The moral thesis about the Fall is again assisted by recourse to a likeness between men and angels, 'God' clearly here as in Genesis—'become as gods' (3: 5, 22)—meaning angels. Just as angels can be deceived by hypocrisy, or sent on apparently irrational errands, so too can they have evil thoughts pass through their minds without coming to moral disaster. The important question is that of approval and consent. It is not the having of the sinful thought but the deliberate indulgence of it and the acting upon it that are sinful. Reason, judgment and the will are the providential remedies against evil thoughts, as also against the appetites and feelings. This is all quite conventional and simple. The complexity of the poem does not consist in a subtle psychological reading of the Fall, but in the subtle logical manipulation of a simple one.

II

Thus Eve's dream, illustrating appetite unchecked by judgment, provides a context in which the forbidden Tree adopts a different, more provocative role. The Tree is not in reality compelling, but, when judgment is in abeyance, it can be shown

132

to seem and to be thought so. This governs the way in which the Tree is presented in the account of the Fall in Book IX. Satan first tells Eve of how he himself had approached the Tree:

Till on a day roaving the field, I chanc'd
A goodly Tree farr distant to behold
Loaden with fruit of fairest colours mixt,
Ruddie and Gold: I neerer drew to gaze;
When from the boughes a savourie odour blow'n,
Grateful to appetite, more pleas'd my sense
Then smell of sweetest Fenel, or the Teats
Of Ewe or Goat dropping with Milk at Eevn,
Unsuckt of Lamb, or Kid, that tend thir play.
To satisfie the sharp desire I had
Of tasting those fair Apples, I resolv'd
Not to deferr; hunger and thirst at once,
Powerful perswaders, quick'nd at the scent
Of that alluring fruit, urg'd me so keene.
(IX, 575-588)

Here, as Satan presents it, the Tree is tempting and irresistible. But he is telling lies about it: when he leads Eve there, it is left significantly undescribed:

So glister'd the dire Snake, and into fraud
Led *Eve* our credulous Mother, to the Tree
Of prohibition, root of all our woe . . .
(IX, 643-645)

and Eve's first recognition of it has nothing of Satan's ecstacy:

To whom thus *Eve* yet sinless Of the Fruit
Of each Tree in the Garden we may eate,
But of the Fruit of this fair Tree amidst
The Garden, God hath said, Ye shall not eate
Thereof, nor shall ye touch it, least ye die.
(IX, 659-663)

The Tree is 'fair' because Genesis said that it was 'good for food and pleasant to the eyes' (3: 6), but the phrase is applied in the most restricted, least intensive way precisely because Eve is 'yet sinless.' But as soon as Eve's mind is swayed by Satan's

133

arguments and her own thoughts, (and not by anything to do with the Tree), then the matter changes:

> He ended, and his words replete with guile
> Into her heart too easie entrance won:
> Fixt on the Fruit she gaz'd, which to behold
> Might tempt alone, and in her ears the sound
> Yet rung of his perswasive words, impregn'd
> With Reason, to her seeming, and with Truth;
> Mean while the hour of Noon drew on, and wak'd
> An eager appetite, rais'd by the smell
> So savourie of that Fruit, which with desire,
> Inclinable now grown to touch or taste,
> Sollicited her longing eye; yet first
> Pausing a while, thus to her self she mus'd.
>
> (IX, 733-744)

This is a most important passage and a model of scrupulous logical thinking. Firstly, the fact that Satan's words 'yet rung' in Eve's ears as she gazed at the Tree shows that the persuasive words and the seeming reason precede the visible attractiveness of the Fruit. This marks the essential point that the inner corruption necessarily came first. The forbidden Fruit has indeed 'Inclinable now grown to touch or taste' because Eve is thinking of eating it. Secondly, in order to press home the point that Eve's possessing appetites in no way indicts God's providence, Milton selects noon as being the time at which Eve fell in order to bring the question of appetite quite aggressively into the matter.[10] This is the climax of an important set of

---

[10] Jackson T. Cope, *The Metaphoric Structure of Paradise Lost* (Baltimore, 1962), pp. 131-137, in a good account of Eve's fall, links Eve's meeting with Satan at noon with Psalm 91: 6 ('the destruction that wasteth at noonday'). He cites Joseph Beaumont's *Psyche* as also making the temptation occur at noon, quoting from the stanza where Satan finds the serpent 'whose illustrious skin/Play'd with the Sun ... all heav'n's highnoon face' (VI, 256). But I think that the full stanza: 'It was the *Serpent*, whose illustrious skin/Play'd with the Sun and sent him back his beams/With glorious use: that Wealth, which glisters in/The proudest strand of oriental Streams,/Salutes Aurora's cheek with fewer raies/Than this bright robe did all heav'n's highnoon face,' merely means that the snake's bright skin shines even against the noonday sun with more brightness than the riches of the East do against the daybreak sun. The noonday reference seems anyway to be part of the description of the snake and not to indicate the time at which the temptation took place.

references and incidents in the poem. The first account of Adam and Eve's life in the Garden includes the 'wholesom thirst and appetite' (IV, 330) that their easy labours raise, 'wholesom' showing that Adam and Eve's having appetites is in itself in no way sinful. God has provided the remedies by which they can be satisfied (food and drink) and controlled (reason). Appetites, a part of Adam and Eve's nature, do not deprive them of their purity or their freedom. Eve's hunger at noon is simply a part of the regimen that God has established in Paradise, the natural and innocent order of work, repast and repose. So Eve, when she leaves Adam, promises to return to him by noon so as 'all things in best order to invite/Noontide repast, or Afternoons repose' (IX, 402-403). The hour of noon is an important part of Milton's system. Nothing will alter the fact that Eve will be hungry at twelve o'clock. She will be hungry whether she meets Satan or not. In the earlier episode of her separation from Adam it was the submissive aspect of Eve's nature that was relevant. Here, at her fall, it is the appetitive. Eve belongs to a certain order of creatures that have appetites, and the one involved here is her hunger.

In order to indicate that this implies no deficiency in her making, Milton again develops a Man-Angel likeness. Angels have already been shown to be like men in that they can be deceived, that evil can come and go in their minds without harm, that their obedience is tested. They are unlike men in that they can fly, that they have direct knowledge of the heavens, that they know by intuition. It is because of the issues raised by Eve's fall that so much emphasis is placed on Raphael's hunger when he visits Adam and Eve, Milton insisting that it is a very real hunger that he feels:

> So down they sat,
> And to thir viands fell, nor seemingly
> The Angel, nor in mist, the common gloss
> Of Theologians, but with keen dispatch
> Of real hunger, and concoctive heate . . .
> (V, 433-437)

Angelic nature, as Raphael himself points out to Adam, carries within it the lower faculties of sense:

> and food alike those pure
> Intelligential substances require
> As doth your Rational; and both contain
> Within them every lower facultie
> Of sense, whereby they hear, see, smell, touch, taste,
> Tasting concoct, digest, assimilate,
> And corporeal to incorporeal turn.
> For know, whatever was created, needs
> To be sustaind and fed . . . (V, 407-415)

Milton's point is not some eccentricity about the materiality of angels but a logical one. He needs Raphael to be very hungry and to turn up in the Garden at the right time for dinner (i.e. noon, see V, 311) because he is looking to the fall of Eve. It helps his point that a creature's hunger affects neither its freedom nor its virtue, that Eve's hunger at noon argues no improvidence on God's part: her hunger is not ungovernable, nor does she have to eat of that particular Tree.

Thirdly, the point that Eve approved her sinful appetite for the wrong Tree is established by the fact that there is a pause between the raising of her appetite and her eating of the Fruit: 'yet first/Pausing a while, thus to her self she mus'd.' This gives her reason the time to consider and her judgment the time to approve or disapprove of the act. The provision of this opportunity for deliberation was necessary, and it was commonplace in the psychology that Milton is using:

> I conceive that in all *deliberations*, that is to say, in an alternate *succession* of contrary *appetites*, the last is that which we call the WILL, & is immediately next before the doing of the action, or next before the doing of it becomes impossible. All other *appetites* to do, and to quit, that come upon a man during his deliberations, are called *Intentions*, & *Inclinations*, but not *Wills*, there being but *one* will, which also in this case may be called the *last* will, though the *Intentions* change often.[11]

[11] Hobbes, *Of Liberty and Necessity* (1954), p. 68-69.

Eve's fall is not possible until her will approves the deed. But as soon as she is resolved in her sin, then Milton can confront her with a very attractive Tree:

> Here grows the cure of all, this Fruit Divine,
> Fair to the Eye, inviting to the Taste,
> Of vertue to make wise . . .
>
> (IX, 776–778)

Like the commentators Milton saw the Genesis account of Eve's fall as being a brief version of what was in fact an extended process. He makes everything hinge on the way in which the phrase 'pleasant to the sight and good for food' is read. Milton takes this to mean two things: (1) fair, and (2) tempting to the appetite. When the phrase is used of the unforbidden trees of the garden, it is used so as to include both senses. But with regard to the forbidden Tree, when Eve first sees that it is good for food and pleasant to the eyes, then the phrase is used in the first sense i.e. fair but not tempting (IX, 661). But when she had decided to eat the forbidden Fruit, then the forbidden Tree became, like all the other trees, fair in a way that includes both senses, i.e. provocative (IX, 736, 777). The process of Eve's fall is marked by a shift of the phrase from one meaning into the other.

It seemed reasonable to suppose that a desire for the forbidden Tree was also a part of Adam's fall. The heavenly view of the Fall does not distinguish between Adam and Eve, and, given the Genesis account:

> 6 And when the woman saw that the tree was good for food, and that it was pleasant to the eyes, and a tree to be desired to make one wise, she took of the fruit thereof, and did eat, and gave also unto her husband with her; and he did eat.
> 7 And the eyes of them both were opened . . .
>
> (Genesis 3)

the fact that the eyes of Adam were ironically opened just as were those of his wife, seemed to imply that his eyes had also at some stage partaken of his Fall. The temptations of appetite

137

and knowledge are thus included also in the fall of Adam, and the same carefulness about the appearance of the Tree is shown with his case. When Adam meets Eve as she hastens to him with a bough of the forbidden Tree

> by the Tree
> Of Knowledge he must pass, there he her met,
> Scarse from the Tree returning; in her hand
> A bough of fairest fruit that downie smil'd,
> New gatherd, and ambrosial smell diffus'd.
> (IX, 848-852)

Milton refrains from describing the Tree itself. That he does extravagantly describe a bough that has been taken from it is perfectly logical: the forbidden Tree is fair as the others trees are, and what Eve is carrying might well be a bough from any tree and hence must be attractive. But as soon as Adam knows what Fruit it is, then it becomes quite flatly the Fruit that they were not to eat:

> how hast thou yeelded to transgress
> The strict forbiddance, how to violate
> The sacred Fruit forbidd'n!
> (IX, 902-904)
> That sacred Fruit, sacred to abstinence . . .
> (IX, 924)

The phrases quite designedly drain away any beauty that there is in the Tree. What next goes on in Adam during his communing with himself is the corruption of the heart, and with that the Tree has nothing at all to do. But as soon as Adam has resolved to join Eve in her sin, then the Tree's aspect changes: 'from the bough/She gave him of that fair enticing Fruit' (IX, 995-996), the addition of 'enticing' to 'fair' showing that the beauty of the Tree is now being presented in the most intensive sense. Adam's hunger is characteristically more self-conscious than Eve's. He is the gourmet as well as the glutton:

138

*Eve*, now I see thou art exact of taste,
And elegant, of Sapience no small part,
Since to each meaning savour we apply,
And Palate call judicious; I the praise
Yeild thee, so well this day thou hast purvey'd.
Much pleasure we have lost, while we abstain'd
From this delightful Fruit, nor known till now
True relish tasting; if such pleasure be
In things to us forbidden, it might be wish'd,
For this one Tree had bin forbidden ten.
But come, so well refrcsh't, now let us play,
As meet is, after such delicious Fare . . .
                              (IX, 1017-1028)

but the Tree attracts only after it has been desired. The enemy
is within.

### III

So although Eve possesses appetites which are natural necessities, although she was bound to be hungry at noon, although
there was a stage in her fall when the forbidden Tree became
provocative, there is no question at all of her being compelled
to sin. This was only the case in her dream when reason and
judgment were in obeyance and when, as the angel held out the
forbidden Fruit to her, it was as though she 'Could not but
taste' (V, 86). But all these factors contribute significantly to
the complication which Milton gives to the case. For if Eve
were compelled to eat, then she would be a figure in a fatalistic
tragedy, which would make the whole episode of her fall a
nice model for the satanic poets who 'complain that Fate/Free
Vertue should enthrall to Force or Chance' (II, 550-551) since
it was by chance that she was found alone, and by necessity
that she ate the Fruit when she stood before the Tree. This
closeness of the matter to satanic tragedy enables Milton to
point up sharply that discrimination between the Christian
and the non-Christian poem which is central to the argument
of *Paradise Lost*. Writing his poem the right way, he knows
fully what would be the wrong.

The satanic subject-matter of 'Free Vertue' plays a very important part in the way in which Milton presents the fall of Eve. The points at issue are freedom and nature. Genesis served to establish the fact that there were different orders of creation: '24 And God said, Let the earth bring forth the living creature after his kind, cattle and creeping thing, and beast of the earth after his kind' (Genesis 1). Man is, as a kind, differentiated from the beasts: he is made in God's image, he has dominion over the other kinds, he is neither a creeping nor a flying thing, marriage is instituted for him alone. Furthermore this concept of Man's ordained and proper kind can be connected with his Fall, since whatever Genesis meant by the idea that the forbidden Fruit would make Man like the gods, it clearly implied Man's becoming what he was not, and what he was not created to be. So Adam and Eve are, in Paradise, free but their nature is none the less a nature within limit. The limitations in Eve's case lie in her being made submissive to Adam, in her having to eat, in her being forbidden to eat of one particular Tree, in her not being able to fly. She exists within the proper restrictions of her nature and her obedience.

Satan's tactic in his temptation of Eve is to replace this Christian 'limited' freedom that Eve has with his own satanic concept of 'Free Vertue.' He argues that Man is not free so long as he lives under *any* sort of restriction, that God's forbidding him the Fruit of the Tree of Knowledge is itself an enthrallment:

> Why then was this forbid? Why but to awe,
> Why but to keep ye low and ignorant,
> His worshippers . . .
>
> (IX, 703-705)

Satan is talking about total freedom. He wants Eve to act in the manner of one who is free to do all things. Furthermore his appeal to Eve's pride, based on what he says to her in Genesis 3: 5 (For God doth know that in the day ye eat thereof, then your eyes shall be opened, and ye shall be as gods, knowing good and evil) offered the opportunity of some elaboration with regard to the question of nature. Satan's flattery of Eve in the poem is subtly addressed to her nature and to her own idea of it:

> Wonder not, sovran Mistress, if perhaps
> Thou canst, who art sole Wonder, much less arm
> Thy looks, the Heav'n of mildness, with disdain,
> Displeas'd that I approach thee thus, and gaze
> Insatiate, I thus single, nor have feard
> Thy awful brow, more awful thus retir'd.
> Fairest resemblance of thy Maker faire,
> Thee all things living gaze on, all things thine
> By gift, and thy Celestial Beautie adore
> With ravishment beheld, there best beheld
> Where universally admir'd; but here
> In this enclosure wild, these Beasts among,
> Beholders rude, and shallow to discerne
> Half what in thee is fair, one man except,
> Who sees thee? (and what is one?) who shouldst be seen
> A Goddess among Gods, ador'd and serv'd
> By Angels numberless, thy daily Train.
>
> (IX, 532-548)

There are a lot of lies and errors in this speech, and Milton offers it as an example of the wrong (though ravishing) love-song which Eve's dream was designed to warn her about. Particularly the speech is constructed to bear upon the Genesis theme of moving outside one's ordained nature, to become like the gods ('a Goddess among Gods'). Extending this into the love song Milton makes Satan's manner of address to Eve form a tight logical knot. The phrase 'sovran Mistress,' deliberately calling into question the pattern which Eve's nature is ordained to have, might make sense in terms of some courtly mode of love, but it is a logical absurdity in the unfallen world of the Garden.'[12] Satan's flattery at first does less than justice to Eve, for wonder she does:

[12] Anne D. Ferry, *Milton's Epic Voice* (Cambridge, Mass., 1963), pp. 141-145 has a good analysis of Satan as fraudulent courtly love poet, noting too the philosophical errors of his speech.

Into the Heart of *Eve* his words made way,
Though at the voice much marveling; at length
Not unamaz'd she thus in answer spake.
(IX, 550-552)

The pressure of literary theory that is so important a force in the poem can be felt very powerfully here. Milton is defining the kind to which his matter seems most appropriately to belong. 'Wonder,' 'marveling,' 'not unamaz'd,' are words that characterize the response to romance as pity and fear characterize the response to tragedy, or admiration to epic. The romance deals with things outside nature, and Eve sees herself as faced with matter of romance since a speaking snake is a wonder, the snake being naturally ordained an inarticulate thing. The point is further stressed in Eve's use of the word 'miracle' in her reply: 'Redouble then this miracle, and say,/ How cam'st thou speakable of mute' (IX, 562-563). She is clearly providentially aware of the differences established between the various orders of creation.

Beginning his temptation with the lover's paradox of 'sovran Mistress,' Satan ends it, close now to Genesis and the idea of becoming as gods, with the suggestion that Eve's nature is even more strikingly paradoxical: 'Goddess humane, reach then, and freely taste' (IX, 732). His 'freely' here indicates that satanic concept of the 'Free vertue' (II, 551), a virtue bold enough to resist the imposition of any limit upon it. The constraints of literary theory serve here to provide Milton with the awareness of the different sorts of poem that his material would make. Satan's 'Free vertue' has its enemy in what he calls 'Fate,' so that when he tells Eve about his own (pretended) eating of the forbidden Fruit, he presents the act to her not as tragedy but as satanic epic.'[13] His aim is to arouse her admiration, not her pity and fear. He has, he says, achieved the heroic deed:

[13] Empson, *Milton's God*, pp. 149-163 seems to me to be very sensitive to Milton's tone here, though I do not agree with his interpretation of its purpose.

> look on mee,
> Mee who have touch'd and tasted, yet both live,
> And life more perfet have attaind then Fate
> Meant mee, by ventring higher than my Lot.
> (IX, 687-690)

This is very characteristic. The venturing is in the high satanic heroic mood. The act is gallantly entered upon in despite of 'Fate' which works against the magnificent aspiration which the free spirit is capable of. 'Lot' in Satan's speech is not something divinely ordained, a proper and not improvident order of nature. It is instead a form of bondage. Satan is claiming to have acted as the typical hero of his own sort of poetry, a satanic epic about 'Thir own heroic deeds' (II, 549), thus bringing into the Garden the ideology and the literature— and these two things are most vitally connected—of the fallen, unredeemed world.[14] The two poems that the situation could yield are brought excitingly close together. Satan presents himself as a figure of pagan epic-heroic, refusing to be thwarted and victimized. Eve on the other hand, is a figure in a Christian epic-free, and subordinate only to a reasonable law. These two

---

[14] Grotius' *Adamus Exul* is interesting at this point in the temptation. Grotius handles the scene very finely, providing Satan with subtle arguments. He also makes him a necessitarian: Satan says to Eve (translations from Kirkconnell):

> For the Fates (*Fata*) control all things.
> We merely do that which has been ordain'd, and suffer
> That which comes down from heav'n.
> (IV, l. 1075-1077)

and he goes on to speak of 'divine necessity' [*dia necessitas*] (IV, l. 1080. See Kirkconnell, p. 161). So, too, when he sees Adam approaching after Eve has eaten the Fruit, he exclaims:

> behold (first omen of thy happy lot [*sortis*] )
> Fit opportunity [*occasio*] has led thy husband hither.
> (IV, l. 1325-1326 [Kirkconnell, p. 175])

Grotius thus uses in the scene the concepts of both chance and necessity. But though he knows his classical drama and its use of such concepts, they are not made systematic and organic in the *Adamus Exul*. Grotius does not, for example, make explicit the idea of chance when Satan finds Eve alone in the Garden. His Satan merely happens upon her without Grotius' seeing the need to look hard at the event.

It is perhaps relevant that Grotius in discussing God's providence in his treatise on *The Truth of the Christian Religion* pays very little attention to discriminating it from chance or necessity.

ways of presenting Eve's choice are part of the two theses about the whole episode of her Fall. The wrong thesis would see the forbidden Tree as made provocative and tempting; it would see Eve, compelled by her hunger, trapped at (of all times) the hour of noon, making the heroic attempt to rise above her lot and to become the god. The right thesis is to see the forbidden Tree as totally indifferent; to see Eve as hungry but not bound to eat of that particular Tree; to see Eve's nature as ordained within limits, but ordained providentially for her good and also, as Raphael tells them (V, 493-503), with the possibility of spiritual growth through obedience; to see her here as simply disobedient.

But once Eve has eaten the Fruit, then the poem moves wholly within the satanic mode. Eve is shifted out of her Christian frame into the pagan one. She is made the total victim, subject not to an appetite which can be controlled by reason, but instead to gluttony, the irrational and uncontrolled sin. Her hunger is now compulsive:

> for *Eve*
> Intent now wholly on her taste, naught else
> Regarded, such delight till then, as seemd,
> In Fruit she never tasted, whether true
> Or fancied so, through expectation high
> Of knowledg, nor was God-head from her thought.
> Greedily she ingorg'd without restraint,
> And knew not eating Death  . .
>
> (IX, 785-792)

This final stage in the process of Eve's fall permits another possible and final reading of the phrase 'good for food and pleasant to the eyes.' The phrase might be taken to imply that, even if there were no provocation in the Tree, nevertheless there was a special delight that belonged to it *after it had been eaten*. The eating of it demonstrably had an effect different from that of the other trees since it brought Death and the knowledge of good and evil. So, with the words 'seemd,' 'whether true or fancied so,' Milton includes the two possibilities. Eve's pleasure was possibly a special and providentially forbidden one that was communicated by the Tree once it was eaten, or it was possibly an ironical cheat of her own sinful fancy. This is the end of the sequence in which Milton has involved his forbidden Tree. In the first stage, before Eve comes to it, it is different from the other trees in that he never describes it at all; in the second stage, as Eve in her process of corruption looks at it, it is the same as the other trees, i.e. fair and tempting; in the third stage, after Eve has eaten of it, Milton allows that it is *perhaps* different in its effect from the other trees, *perhaps* special and more delightful. The nature of the Tree is made to wait upon Eve's will and deed. The logical pressure of the account splits the Genesis phrase into a variety of meaning.

The irony implicit in the outcome in Genesis, that Eve's eyes were opened only to an awareness of her own nakedness, allows of some extension. Besides playing a trick upon her knowledge, the Fruit is in the poem also made to play a trick upon her nature. Eve had hoped by eating it to become like the gods, an 'expectation high.' But the Fruit confers the angelic privilege of flight only deceitfully. The only heightening that Eve achieves is (punningly) that of drunkenness: 'hight'nd as with Wine, jocond and boon,' (IX, 793), and later, with Adam, she merely *seems* to fly:

> They swim in mirth, and fansie that they feel
> Divinitie within them breeding wings
> Wherewith to scorne the Earth . . .
> (IX, 1009-1011)

Moreover a sinister heroic note sounds in the speech which Eve makes to Adam when they meet:

> I
> Have also tasted, and have also found
> Th'effects to correspond, opener mine Eyes,
> Dimm erst, dilated Spirits, ampler Heart,
> And growing up to Godhead; which for thee

Chiefly I sought, without thee can despise.
For bliss, as thou hast part, to me is bliss,
Tedious, unshar'd with thee, and odious soon.
Thou therefore also taste, that equal Lot
May joyne us, equal Joy, as equal Love;
Least thou not tasting, different degree
Disjoyne us, and I then too late renounce
Deitie for thee, when Fate will not permit.
                                    (IX, 873-885)

With its irrational yearning and its apparent self-sacrifice,
this is a satanic speech. Eve is being made to act up a new role
(for her) of pagan epic hero. Her reference to 'Fate' is Godless;
her use of 'Lot' discontented and absurd. And she sees her act
within a different framework of implication, as an example of
the wrong literary kind. When, in her dream, she had seen the
angel pluck the forbidden Fruit, she had seen it as a tragedy:

This said he paus'd not, but with ventrous Arme
He pluckt, he tasted; mee damp horror chil'd
As such bold words voucht with a deed so bold . . .
                                    (V, 64-66)

The boldness and venture of the act had not led the unfallen
Eve into thinking it epic (rousing admiration). She had properly
felt horror as at a tragic spectacle. Now, looking at her own
act after her fall, she gets it wrong. Her speech to Adam
strikes the note of reckless self-sacrifice. Adam does not miss
that note:

Bold deed thou hast presum'd, adventrous *Eve*,
And peril great provok't, who thus hath dar'd . . .
                                    (IX, 921-922)

'Bold,' 'adventrous,' 'peril,' 'dar'd' show Adam's sensitivity
to the epic quality that Eve claims for her deed. The constraints, logical and literary, within which she now sees herself
as moving, are those of Hell.

Thus the Genesis idea of becoming like gods gave Milton

the 'argument' for the pagan epic which is hidden in Book IX. It provided the occasion for an important incursion into literary theory. Milton deliberately contrived a collision between the Christian and pagan ideologies and literary kinds and at the fall of Eve transformed one mode into the other. The moral upheaval in Eve's world at her fall is marked by a corresponding upheaval in ideological and literary terms.

## IV

Milton came to the fall of Eve with a sharp awareness of how it could be made to seem a tragedy of necessity, and to further his insistence that it was not that sort of tragedy he came back to the point later in the poem, arranging a demonstration of what Eve's fall would look like if she had really been picked out by God as his victim. For if she had been so picked out and necessitated, then she would have been reprobate, and what the tragedy of the reprobate is like we are shown in Book X. Milton's account of the transformation scene in Hell presents precisely the sort of tragedy that he does not want us to see in Book IX. Acted out in Hell is the tragedy of doom, its heroes the damned. In the midst of their applause for Satan's success with Man, the devils are turned suddenly into snakes and a fair prospect of trees is set before them:

> There stood
> A Grove hard by, sprung up with this thir change,
> His will who reigns above, to aggravate
> Thir penance, laden with fair Fruit like that
> Which grew in Paradise, the bait of *Eve*
> Us'd by the Tempter . . .
>
> (X, 547–552)

Here is the provocative Fruit, and Milton tells us squarely what the provocation implies about God's will. If it is his will to tempt his creatures so irresistibly, then it is his will that they fall. But God had earlier in the poem denied that this was his intent with regard to Man:

147

I formd them free, and free they must remain,
Till they enthrall themselves: I else must change
Thir nature, and revoke the high Decree
Unchangeable, Eternal, which ordain'd
Thir freedom, they themselves ordain'd thir fall.
(III, 124-128)

This speech is about the central issues of the poem. If God had
ordained the Fall, then the tragedy of Man in Book IX would
be like that of the devils in Book X. The provocation of the
Fruit would then properly be called 'a will to aggravate.'
Man would be fallen and transformed before he came to the
forbidden Tree just as the devils are turned into snakes before
they do. In his nature Man, as the devils are, would be compelled, not free:

Yet parcht with scalding thurst and hunger fierce,
Though to delude them sent, could not abstain,
But on they rould in heaps, and up the Trees
Climbing, sat thicker then the snakie locks
That curld *Megaera*: greedily they pluck'd
The Frutage fair to sight, like that which grew
Neer that bituminous Lake where *Sodom* flam'd;
This more delusive, not the touch, but taste
Deceav'd; they fondly thinking to allay
Thir appetite with gust, instead of Fruit
Chewd bitter Ashes, which th'offended taste
With spattering noise rejected: oft they assayd,
Hunger and thirst constraining, drugd as oft,
With hatefullest disrelish writh'd thir jaws
With soot and cinders fill'd; so oft they fell
Into the same illusion, not as Man
Whom they triumph'd once lapst. Thus were they plagu'd
And worn with Famin, long and ceasless hiss . . .
X, 556-573)

Here are figures in the grip of appetites which they find it
impossible to control, mocked by an alluring and deceitful
Tree. In Hell the fairness of the Tree is thus a ghastly irony from

the start. It is ironical in the earthly Garden only after human freedom and decision have had their say. The scene in Book X thus provides a beautiful model of the satanic necessitated tragedy. This tragedy, if God is provident, cannot be the truth about Man's fall, and Milton has been careful not to write it in Book IX. It has satanic heroes and a satanic disposition of plot and argument, and in Hell therefore it finds its proper theatre.

# 8

# The Fall of Adam

## I

MARRIAGE is the crucial issue in the fall of Adam and since this was an institution established by God for Man before the Fall, Genesis itself could be used to throw some light on Adam's case. Furthermore the institution was one about which Milton himself had showed much concern in his writings, so the matter had an especial interest for him. Genesis provides the following texts:

> 27 So God created man in his own image, in the image of God created he him; male and female created he them.
> 28 And God blessed them, and God said unto them, Be fruitful and multiply, and replenish the earth . . .
>
> (Genesis 1)
>
> 18 And the LORD God said, It is not good that the man should be alone; I will make him an help meet for him.
>
> 23 And Adam said, This is now bone of my bones, and flesh of my flesh: she shall be called Woman, because she was taken out of Man.
> 24 Therefore shall a man leave his father and his mother and, shall cleave unto his wife: and they shall be one flesh.
>
> (Genesis 2)

The meaning of some of these things and the relationship between them are of course very difficult to establish, but

Milton's prose shows that he thought that he knew what they meant and what their relationship to each other was. On his view the establishment of marriage for the procreation of children in Genesis 1 had to be seen in the light of what was said in the even more crucial Genesis 2. Since beasts also had offspring, it was the second chapter that defined fully the uniquely human institution. Firstly, in what God said, it could be seen that marriage was provided for the solace of loneliness and for mutual comfort. Secondly, in the words of Adam, marriage set up an especial oneness of the flesh between a husband and wife and hence sanctified that sexual link which is referred to in Genesis 1: 27: 'male and female created he them.' So a marriage has three possible means of justifying itself: it has produced children, it provides mutual solace, a man and his wife are one in the flesh. There are clearly various possibilities here: a married couple might have children but still be no comfort to each other, or a couple might mutually cherish each other but be childless. The question naturally arises as to the point at which a marriage is a marriage in name only and hence dissoluble, and this was a question that Milton spent much time arguing out in his divorce tracts. In particular he was concerned with the two aspects of marriage as defined in the second chapter of Genesis, solace and oneness in the flesh, and concerned to insist on the first as the more important of the two. It was after all God's own statement about the institution, and in its concern for Man's happiness it was more provident and rational. Moreover it gave Milton the grounds for his arguments about divorce since a man might conceivably find that his comfort was better served by his leaving his wife than by his staying with her. It was especially irritating to Milton that divorce was allowed in cases where a marriage did not succeed in establishing a oneness in the flesh (e.g. non-consummation, etc.) but not in cases where it did not succeed in establishing a oneness in the spirit (see *Tetrachordon*, IV, 88-90). In his view Adam's definition of the nature of marriage, being human merely, had to be seen as subordinate to God's.

It certainly could not supersede God's, nor run counter to it. He argues indeed in *Tetrachordon* that Adam's words may be no more than a repetition of God's, a repetition reflecting Adam's concern with the physical aspect of the institution as God's own words reflected the spiritual:

> But if in these words we shall make *Adam* to erect a new establish-ment of mariage in the meer flesh, which God so lately had instituted, and founded in the sweet and mild familiarity of love and solace and mutuall fitnes, what do we but use the mouth of our generall parent, the first time it opens, to an arrogant op-position, and correcting of God's wiser ordinance. These words therefore cannot import any thing new in mariage, but either that which belongs to *Adam* only, or to us in reference only to the instituting words of God which made a meet help against lonelines. *Adam* spake like *Adam* the words of flesh and bones, the shell and rinde of matrimony; but God spake like God, of love and solace and meet help, the soul both of *Adams* words and of matrimony.
>
> (*Tetrachordon*, IV, 93)

God's own purpose in the institution needs to be looked to. The sexual link of nature is not the prime cause of marriage. It was because he thought this that Milton showed some concern at St Paul's blunt recommendation of marriage as a means to avoid fornication since he thought that it spoke too slightingly of a relationship whose basis is essentially reason and law (see *Tetrachordon*, IV, 167-168). He was equally worried over St Paul's 'It is better to marry than to burn' (I Corinthians: 7, 9), and argues in the *Doctrine and Discipline of Divorce* that marriage is not the only remedy for the stings of physical desire that a provident God has provided: there are also 'strict life and labour with the abatement of a full diet' (III, Part II, 397) and, given the intellectual burning that comes from an ill-matched marriage (a burning that nothing will allay) it may sometimes be better to divorce than to burn.

The first presentation of the institution in *Paradise Lost* is made in the light of what is said in Genesis 1: 27, 28:

Our Maker bids increase, who bids abstain
But our Destroyer, foe to God and Man?
Haile wedded Love, mysterious Law, true sourse
Of Human ofspring, sole proprietie,
In Paradise of all things common else.
By thee adulterous lust was driv'n from men
Among the bestial herds to raunge, by thee
Founded in Reason, Loyal, Just, and Pure,
Relations dear, and all the Charities
Of Father, Son, and Brother first were known.

$$\text{(IV, 748-757)}$$

but starting with God's command to increase and multiply
Milton goes beyond Genesis in order to insist on the rational
and moral basis of the institution. Given this, sexuality in Man
is made pure (as exemplified in the scenes of unfallen love in the
Garden). Without it the sexual appetite is no more than what
unites beasts in the animal kingdom. This important point is
taken up and developed in Adam's discussion with Raphael
about the marriage relationship in Book VIII. Adam tells
Raphael that his delight in Eve is of a different nature from
the delight that he finds in other things:

and must confess to find
In all things else delight indeed, but such
As us'd or not, works in the mind no change,
Nor vehement desire, these delicacies
I mean of Taste, Sight, Smell, Herbs, Fruits, and Flours,
Walks, and the melodie of Birds; but here
Farr otherwise, transported I behold,
Transported touch; here passion first I felt,
Commotion strange, in all enjoyments else
Superiour and unmov'd, here onely weake
Against the charm of Beauties powerful glance.

$$\text{(VIII, 523-533)}$$

Crucial words here which vibrate across *Paradise Lost* and
across Milton's other writings are 'vehement' and 'charm.
Vehemence, which belongs to Chaos (II, 954) and is used in

the *Argument* to Book IX specifically in connection with Adam's fall ('Adam . . . *resolves through vehemence of love to perish with her*') stresses the strength and irrationality of Adam's feeling, its mindlessness (*ve* + *mens*); and 'charm' (used in II, 556 to describe the devils' eloquence) indicates that which moves the emotions and lulls the reason. But these are dangerous words for Adam to use about an institution that is founded upon reason, and Raphael in his reply goes on to interpret Adam's strange delight very simply:

> But if the sense of touch whereby mankind
> Is propagated seem such dear delight
> Beyond all other, think the same voutsaf't
> To Cattel and each Beast; which would not be
> To them made common and divulg'd, if aught
> Therein enjoy'd were worthy to subdue
> The Soule of Man, or passion in him move.
>
> (VIII, 579-585)

This might seem a rather brutal reading of Adam's case, but Raphael is merely spelling out what Milton has himself said in his invocation to wedded love earlier in the poem and had argued extensively in his prose. Since sexuality is common to beasts and to men, marriage, which is an institution ordained for man alone, is not simply the institution of sexuality for man. Raphael's point is that wedded love is in its true nature rational as he goes on to say:

> What higher in her societie thou findst
> Attractive, human, rational, love still;
> In loving thou dost well, in passion not,
> Wherein true Love consists not; love refines
> The thoughts, and heart enlarges, hath his seat
> In Reason, and is judicious . . .
>
> (VIII, 586-591)

The discrimination between love and passion is altogether conventional, but it is characteristically backed up in Milton by a lot of theory. True love is reasonable, whereas Raphael offers a very narrow reading of passion, seeing it simply as sexual appetite. There is no need to suppose that Milton himself thought this a misrepresentation of the matter. In the words of *Tetrachordon* quoted earlier, Adam is speaking 'the words of flesh and bones, the shell and rinde of matrimony' (IV, 93), and Adam goes on to accept and develop Raphael's view of the case:

> Neither her out-side formd so fair, nor aught
> In procreation common to all kindes
> (Though higher of the genial Bed by far,
> And with mysterious reverence I deem)
> So much delights me as those graceful acts,
> Those thousand decencies that daily flow
> From all her words and actions mixt with Love
> And sweet compliance, which declare unfeign'd
> Union of Mind, or in us both one Soule;
> Harmonie to behold in wedded pair
> More grateful than harmonious sound to the eare.
> Yet these subject not; I to thee disclose
> What inward thence I feel, not therefore foild,
> Who meet with various objects, from the sense
> Variously representing; yet still free
> Approve the best, and follow what I approve.
>
> (VIII, 596-611)

The insistence on approval shows the necessity of judgment in marriage. It shows also that Adam in this previous speech is not already fallen since the error there is not approved. As Eve's dream was intended as a providential warning for her, so is Adam's discussion with Raphael a warning for him. His fall is shown not in his feeling or admitting to passion, but in his submitting to it.

Adam is, in his speech, explaining to Raphael what his response to Eve is, not as she is a woman, but as she is his wife. He is prepared, like Raphael, to see the link of nature as the link of 'procreation common to all kinds' though one made especially high in the case of Man because of the divine

155

institution within which it was enjoyed. But, as his wife, Eve provides delights that arise out of their domestic community of life, so that the relationship of husband and wife is a union in the widest possible sense. The Adam of Genesis says of it that 'they shall be one flesh,' but Milton's Adam sees a significantly wider union: it is a 'Union of Mind, or in us both one Soule,' and his version of the definition of marriage in Genesis 2: 24 contains the same important additions:

> I now see
> Bone of my Bone, Flesh of my Flesh, my Self
> Before me; Woman is her Name, of Man
> Extracted; for this cause he shall forgoe
> Father and Mother, and to his Wife adhere;
> And they shall be one Flesh, one Heart, one Soule.
>
> (VIII, 494-499)

The addition of mind and heart and soul to the union which marriage provides shows Milton crucially redefining that oneness which, in Genesis, is of the flesh only.

The discourse with Raphael presents marriage in the light that is cast on what is said in Genesis 1: 27, 28 by what is said in Genesis 2: 18, 23, 24. The link of nature is made subordinate to the solace which the union of man and wife provides. Milton clearly has the highest possible view of the institution. It is a contract reasonably instituted and reasonably entered upon, involving a just and full consciousness of the duties and responsibilities of each partner to the other. Utterly Miltonic is the sense of conduct as arising from a set of obligations nicely balanced and judged. It was here for example that Dalila's error was shown, Samson arguing that her love for him, if it had been sincere, would have involved a proper consciousness in her of her duties towards him as her husband:

> But had thy love, still odiously pretended,
> Bin, as it ought, sincere, it would have taught thee
> Far other reasonings, brought forth other deeds . . .
>
> (Samson, 873-875)

She should in particular have recognized that her obligations to her husband superseded those of her country:

> if aught against my life
> Thy countrey sought of thee, it sought unjustly,
> Against the law of nature, law of nations . . .
>
> *(Samson,* 888-890)

What can look legalistic in Milton is merely an important aspect of his insistence upon reason and judgment.

## II

That Adam fell because he was captivated by Eve's charm was a natural and commonplace way of reading what happened at his fall:

> But because Moses simply relates that he ate the fruit taken from the hands of his wife, the opinion has been commonly received, that he was rather captivated with her allurements than persuaded by Satan's impostures. For this purpose the declaration of Paul is adduced, 'Adam was not deceived, but the woman,' (I Tim. ii. 14.) But Paul in that place, as he is teaching that the origin of evil was from the woman, only speaks comparatively. Indeed, it was not only for the sake of complying with the wishes of his wife that he transgressed the law laid down for him; but being drawn by her into fatal ambition, he became partaker of the same defection with her. And truly Paul elsewhere states that sin came not by the woman, but by Adam himself. (Rom. v. 12.) Then, the reproof which soon afterwards follows, 'Behold, Adam is as one of us,' clearly proves that he also foolishly coveted more then was lawful, and gave greater credit to the flatteries of the devil, than to the sacred word of God.[1]

Calvin's explication of the Fall here shows the tight limits within which it was necessary to work. His concern is for a coherent account, Genesis, St Paul and reason all needing to be made consistent with each other. Milton also did not miss much

---

[1] Calvin, *Commentaries upon Genesis,* trans. King, I, 152.

where this sort of thing was in question, and he offers a very distinguished logical appraisal of the episode.

His first problem was with the nature of Adam's fall. The fact that Adam fell through his wife's allurements made it reasonable to suppose that there was some sexual element involved in his fall, especially when Genesis said that the first effect of the forbidden Fruit was Adam and Eve's sense of their own nakedness. But it could not be supposed that the sexual appetite was itself a guilty thing. God himself had before the Fall commanded Man to increase and multiply, and so sexuality was necessarily created pure:

> Whatever Hypocrites austerely talk
> Of puritie and place and innocence,
> Defaming as impure what God declares
> Pure, and commands to som, leaves free to all.
> Our Maker bids increase, who bids abstain
> But our destroyer, foe to God and Man?
>
> (IV, 744-749)

Milton, in Adam's discourse with Raphael, presents the appetite as common (i.e. shared by beasts) because he wishes to establish it as a secondary part of marriage. But he must also insist that it is, for Man within marriage, innocent. The scenes of innocent physical love-making between Adam and Eve help to establish this, but to help out the thesis Milton again has recourse to a Man-Angel likeness, and presents angelic sexuality for the same reason that he presents angelic hunger, although he naturally finds it a bit more awkward. He makes his point at the end of Adam's dialogue with Raphael when Adam asks Raphael directly if angels love. Raphael's blush at the question ('Loves proper hue' (VIII, 619)) is, like Eve's, the blush of innocent modesty, of pure and private sexuality. This connects sex usefully with marriage and further does not much encourage more questions about the matter. This suits Milton very well. We do not learn whether angels marry, or what sort of sex life they really enjoy. Milton wants merely to establish angelic sexuality without ever getting very specific about it. The details did not interest him since his purpose was simply to set up part of his logical case about the Fall. So Raphael's warnings to Adam about sexuality do not imply that the appetite is itself immoral or impure since the appetite turns out to be possessed by the angel himself. Thus before he comes to the episode of Adam's fall, Milton has already made it clear that it was not simply Man's possession of sexual appetites that was responsible for his fall, since that would be to indict the providence of God who had created Man's particular nature.

His second problem was with the manner in which Adam's resolve to join Eve in her sin was made. It was necessary to present that resolve as combining insight with speed. The insight is shown in that Adam was not deceived when he fell. St Paul had said that he was not deceived: '14 And Adam was not deceived, but the woman being deceived was in the transgression' (I Timothy 2); and the logic of the case anyway insisted that Adam could not be deceived since that would argue that God had given him insufficient wisdom for his situation, and hence that God was not provident. (Eve's understanding on the other hand can be allowed to be deceived since Adam was her protector in such cases.) So, as soon as Eve tells Adam that she has eaten the forbidden Fruit, he fully understands her error, seeing her deed as a tragic spectacle, an image of horror:

> On th'other side, *Adam*, soon as he heard
> The Fatal Trespass don by *Eve*, amaz'd,
> Astonied stood and Blank, while horror chill
> Ran through his veins, and all his joynts relax'd . . .
> (IX, 888-891)

and he is under no illusions about the nature of his own sinful act: 'he scrupled not to eat/Against his better knowledge, not deceav'd' (IX, 997-998). Milton is necessarily here following St Paul and the logical requirements of the case. That is why the real awkwardness in Milton's account is earlier in the book, where Adam, letting Eve depart to garden alone, is more deceived than he should have been. But it was better to have Adam deceived there—where a set of very persuasive arguments could be provided—than here where it would be obviously disastrous, slighting to God and contrary to St Paul. Milton's Adam is very undeceived indeed. His surmise about what might have happened to Eve, 'Som cursed fraud/Of Enemie hath beguil'd thee, yet unknown' (IX, 904-905), is the truth, and his understanding of what their sin involves for himself and his wife is clear.

If Adam cannot be deceived, then it follows that he cannot be persuaded to eat the forbidden Fruit. Persuasion to do the wrong thing must be deceitful. Many of the other literary versions of the Fall go wrong at this point. Eve in *Genesis B* spends all day pleading for Adam to join her in her sin and he finally consents.[2] Grotius's Adam finds that 'to choose is hard,'[3] Dryden's Adam too is heroically torn:

> Hard state of life! since Heaven foreknows my will,
> Why am I not tied up from doing ill?[4]

asking a question full of more difficulty than Dryden sees. Eve in the *Adamo Caduto* also attempts persuasion and finally beguiles Adam into sin by flattery, another form of persuasion.[5] These accounts, many of them not unmoving, pay insufficient regard to the logic of the matter. Persuasion must fail with Adam since there can be no good reason for doing the wrong thing. If there were, then no one would see it more clearly than Adam himself. Furthermore, even if attempted persuasions fail, as they must, the inclusion of them at length courts trouble since it makes the eventual fall of Adam all the more difficult to bring off. The more his decision to eat the forbidden Fruit is delayed, the more difficult does it become to understand.

[2] l. 684.
[3] *Adamus Exul*, Act IV. (Trans. Kirkconnell, *The Celestial Cycle*, p. 183).
[4] *State of Innocence*, IV, i.
[5] Act II, sc. X. (See Kirkconnell, p. 329.)

The longer Adam is made to think about it, the more resolved should he become not to do it.

Adam's resolve therefore must be made speedily, so speedily that it barely needs to be thought out. But this speed has necessarily to be combined with insight and responsibility. For if Adam acted purely out of instinct, without deliberation and understanding, then the blame for his fall would be not his but God's. Adam might have fallen because of what Calvin called 'the allurements of his wife' rather than because of any arguments, but the responsibility for yielding to those feelings must still be his. This is why Adam's schooling by Raphael in the previous book is so important. Given that previous exercise in discrimination about his feelings towards his wife, the immediateness of his act here when faced with the same issues does not excuse it. The act is then still a free and responsible one. Hobbes takes the same view about apparently impulsive acts:

> Besides, I see 'tis reasonable to punish a *rash* Action, which could not be justly done by man to man, unless the same were *voluntarie*. For no *action* of a man can be said to be without *deliberation*, though never so sudden, because it is supposed he had time to *deliberate* all the precedent time of his life, whether he should do that kind of action or not. And hence it is, that he that killeth in a sudden passion of *Anger*, shall nevertheless be justly put to *death*, because all the time, wherein he was able to consider, whether to kill were good or evil, shall be held for one continual *deliberation*, and consequently the killing shall be judged to proceed from *election*.[6]

This view is the only possible one for Milton to adopt if he is to make sense of the Fall and justify God's providence. The 'precedent time' for deliberation which Hobbes supposes is, in Adam's case, not at all hypothetical since Raphael has previously taken him step by step over the issues involved. This is one reason why the means by which Adam is warned are so much more argumentative and theoretical than those

[6] *Of Liberty and Necessity*, p. 66-67.

that warn his wife. Even so, Adam is given some token time before his resolve is made:

> Speechless he stood and pale, till thus at length
> First to himself he inward silence broke.
>
> (IX, 894-895)

but Milton does not say how long that time was or what he deliberated. The whole tactic consists in making Adam's decision slow enough not to seem instinct and fast enough not to make it seem the outcome of a process of careful argument. Importantly Adam had the opportunity to withdraw. Milton is thus brought inexorably to

> he scrupl'd not to eat
> Against his better knowledge, not deceav'd,
> But fondly overcome with Femal charm.
>
> (IX, 997-999)

as his account of the manner of Adam's fall.

Once Adam has resolved to eat the Fruit, then what follows is not reason but rationalization. Adam's long speech with himself is consequent upon a decision already made, not a prelude to a decision. This is how it is presented in the *Argument* to Book IX: 'Adam *at first amaz'd, but perceiving her lost, resolves through vehemence of love to perish with her; and extenuating the trespass, eats also of the Fruit*' and because Adam has now acquiesced in his fall, the speech can safely show the corruption of his judgment. So this is where Milton can properly include the Genesis material of the Fruit, the eating of which leads to godhead. Adam looks on the Tree as something that will transform his nature: 'to be Gods, or Angels Demi-gods' (IX, 937); and the Tree itself becomes an object of pleasure, 'fair enticing Fruit' (IX, 996). The arguments about godhead would have received short shrift from Adam before his resolve to join Eve was made, nor were his senses then aroused by the forbidden Tree. But the arguments now properly act as justifications rather than motives, and the Tree is attractive to him because his decision to eat its Fruit is already taken.

162

III

Milton's third problem with the fall of Adam is to look hard at its implications with respect to his thesis about God's providence. The whole episode is managed with great warmth of feeling and human interest, but for all the emotional complexity that it has the situation is still fundamentally one which reduces to a choice between two courses of action, to eat or not to eat the forbidden Fruit, and from the point of view of his thesis Milton must think that the choice that Adam eventually made was not right but wrong.[7] So the scene has to be looked at in its theoretical as well as its emotional context, and this theoretical context is very elaborate. Milton's comment that Adam was 'fondly overcome with Femal charm' (IX, 999) points us back to the discussion with Raphael about the 'charm of Beauties powerful glance' (VIII, 533) and also to Genesis on which that discussion is based. As the word 'Femal' shows, he is looking to the terms in which marriage was instituted: '27 . . . male and female created he them' (Genesis 1) because he is concerned with how what he is describing here fits into the institution of marriage as it was ordained by God for Adam and Eve. God's intention was solace and not charm, so for Adam to act 'fondly' (i.e. without reason as well as with feeling), for him to indulge the irrationality that the word 'charm' implies, is for Adam to act contrary to the good of his own nature and of the institution. In yielding to the sexual nature of Eve's appeal, her 'Femal charm,' Adam is, as Milton sees it, making the lesser part of marriage, the link of nature, take precedence over the greater one of solace and mutual comfort. In the light of this Adam's final resolution is written and commented on with great deliberation:

[7] For the case that Adam did the right thing, see especially Waldock, *Paradise Lost and its Critics*, pp. 46–57. Ferry, *Milton's Epic Voice*, pp. 56–65 differentiates very sensitively the different points of view and tone in the episode and makes the point that it is Adam's sin to suppose that his choice is inevitable. She also notes the satanic vocabulary at the close of Adam's speech. My own line is that there is a lot more theory to Adam's case than has often been supposed.

for with thee
Certain my resolution is to Die;
How can I live without thee, how forgoe
Thy sweet Converse and Love so dearly joyn'd,
To live again in these wilde Woods forlorn?
Should God create another *Eve*, and I
Another Rib afford, yet loss of thee
Would never from my heart; no, no, I feel
The Link of Nature draw me: Flesh of Flesh,
Bone of my Bone thou art, and from thy State
Mine never shall be parted, bliss or woe.
(IX, 906-916)

The beauty of these lines is part of Milton's design since he is putting a 'romantic' case as strongly as he can, exemplifying in the warm tone of the speech the passion of Adam's fall. The immediate response which they arouse, our sense of a heart-felt case being made, is all expected and contrived. But Milton knows also that this is only one way of looking at Adam's case, one 'poem' to be written about it. Even if we are moved, Adam must be wrong. If the speech is attractive, then so are the songs of Hell:

Thir Song was partial, but the harmony
(What could it less when Spirits immortal sing?)
Suspended Hell, and took with ravishment
The thronging audience.
(II, 552-555)

On Milton's view Adam's heroic mood, his sense of surrender and self-sacrifice, is a fallen satanic one, and therefore finds its suitable expression in a fallen satanic mode of mere 'charm.'

Deliberately creating a poetry of emotion, Milton expects us to look also to the logic of what Adam says. Adam is justifying his act, and justifying it in terms of the institution of marriage. He claims firstly that he cannot live alone without Eve, and in this he is apparently justified by what God had said about marriage when he instituted it: 'And the LORD God said, It is not good that man should be alone; I will make him an help meet for him' (Genesis 2: 18). Adam's case is that by joining Eve in her sin he is enabled to avoid that state of loneliness which she had at the first been created to dispel, and that to lose her 'sweet Converse and Love' is to deprive himself of that solace for the provision of which marriage was ordained. This case would make his decision the right one in terms of God's providence which had given him Eve in the beginning. But Milton must clearly think that this argument is absurd since he had in his prose writings been much concerned to refute it. His arguments for divorce were based upon the need to discriminate carefully between the true and false modes of solace in marriage. He saw a man and wife as firmly bound together only so long as they lived within the solace of a truly Christian marriage. It is in this context that Adam's case must be seen. God's intention with marriage was to provide for Man the means of happiness, and this involved, with a rational creature, Man's own recognition of a set of duties and obligations. Adam's first duty is that of obedience to God so it is impossible for him to claim as he does that the remedying of his loneliness should take priority over the command not to eat of the forbidden Tree. Furthermore there was a ladder of solace in marriage: 'in matrimony there must be first a mutuall help to piety, next to civill fellowship of love and amity, then to generation, so to household affairs, lastly the remedy of incontinence' (*Tetrachordon*, IV, 88). In the light of this carefully ranked welfare Adam's error in the poem is obvious. His resolve to join Eve is an offence against the first, for the eating of the Fruit is an impious act. And it does not lead to love and amity for its outcome is death and despair. There can be no true society in sinfulness. The upshot of the Fall, Adam and Eve's quarrel and mutual recriminations, provides a logical and ironical end to what Adam is here calling their 'sweet Converse and Love.' Solace is what Adam had quite properly looked forward to in his meeting with Eve at noon:

Great joy he promis'd to his thoughts, and new
Solace in her return, so long delay'd . . .
(IX, 843-844)

but confronted with Eve in her sin Adam gets confused as to
where his solace really lies. Eve, trying to lead him into sin in
offering him the forbidden Fruit, has offended against the idea
of solace. So any solace that he hopes to find by sharing her
sin is deceitful. Hence Milton's sarcastic use of the word after
the Fall:

There they thir fill of Love and Loves disport
Took largely, of thir mutual guilt the Seale,
The solace of thir sin . . .
(IX, 1042-1044)

Their only solace has become a mockery. When it was too late
Adam himself was prepared to look harder at the concept of
solace that he had erroneously entertained: 'This Woman
whom thou mad'st to be my help/ . . . Shee gave me of the
Tree, and I did eate' (X, 137 . . . 143). But the confusion about
his solace was his and not God's.

Adam, in his speech, makes a second serious error when, at
its close, he bases the justification of his resolve to join Eve
upon the link of nature that he has with her:

I feel
The Link of Nature draw me: Flesh of Flesh,
Bone of my Bone thou Art . . .
(IX, 913-915)

This is to rest his case upon what Milton (and Raphael)
regards as the subordinate element in marriage. It involves a
radical lessening of the grounds of their union. In Book VIII
Milton, as discussed earlier in this chapter, had significantly
extended the oneness in the flesh of Genesis to 'one Flesh, one
Heart, one Soule' (VIII, 499), but Adam now has merely
'Flesh of Flesh/Bone of my Bone,' and in his next speech
'we are one,/One Flesh' (IX, 958-959). The oneness in marriage

that Adam lays claim to has been sharply and disastrously
reduced, and it is irrational for Adam to justify his marriage by
invoking it:

> In like manner heer, *They shall be one flesh*; but let the causes
> hold, and be made really good, which only have the possibility
> to make them one flesh. Wee know that flesh can neither joyn,
> nor keep together two bodies of it self; what is it then must
> make them one flesh, but liknes, but fitnes of mind and disposition,
> which may breed the Spirit of concord, and union between them?
> If that be not in the nature of either, and that there has bin a
> remediles mistake, as vain wee goe about to compell them into
> one flesh, as if wee undertook to weav a garment of drie sand.
>
> (*Tetrachordon*, IV, 97)

This provides the refutation of Adam's case. The link of
nature cannot be used to justify a situation which offends
against the ideas of good, of solace and of reason. Standing
finally to nature. Adam is denying the true end of marriage.
Nature is no Christian justification: 'The power of nature is a
good plea for those that acknowledge nothing above nature.
But it is not an excuse for a Christian.'[8] This concept of
marriage as founded upon the link of nature and the oneness
of the flesh was the one that Milton had fought most bitterly
in his divorce writings, and his making Adam adopt it shows
how little he endorses Adam's case. He gets some revenge upon
it too by showing that as a link it has its satanic counterpart,
since it is shared also by Satan, Sin and Death. The infamous
trinity of Hell is united by what the *Argument* to Book X
ironically calls '*wondrous sympathie*,' a link that the poem
expands:

> Methinks I feel new strength with me rise,
> Wings growing, and Dominion giv'n me large
> Beyond the Deep; whatever drawes me on,
> Or sympathie, or som connatural force
> Powerful at greatest distance to unite
> With secret amity things of like kinde

[8] Joseph Hall, *Heaven upon Earth*, (*Works*, p. 80.)

By secretest conveyance. Thou my Shade
Inseparable must with mee along;
For Death from Sin no power can separate.

(X, 243-251)

In what is a grim parody of Adam's speech, Sin makes the same claim about the link of nature. So even if the oneness in the flesh was an especial one in the case of Adam and Eve since Eve was made from Adam's body, that gives it no moral force. The relationship between Satan, Sin and Death is of that order too: Sin, sprang from Satan's head and Death is their child. The fact that Milton set up a Man-Devil likeness in respect to this particular issue shows how anxious he was to put it in its place. It is much to his credit that he does not, (unlike Dante), put persons in his Hell, but he puts ideas there to some purpose.

Milton is thus playing devil's advocate in his making of Adam's case. It is related to the theory of marriage about which he himself cared very deeply. This is why the comment which he goes on to make about Adam's situation is so important:

So having said, as one from sad dismay
Recomforted, and after thoughts disturbd
Submitting to what seemd remediless,
Thus in calm mood his Words to *Eve* he turnd.

(IX, 917-920)

The word 'remediless' is vital. For Adam to claim that his situation is without remedy calls into question that providence of God which it is the poem's purpose to justify. The situation without remedy is a situation of despair, and Milton's saying that Adam's situation 'seemd remediless' shows that he does not endorse Adam's claim. C. S. Lewis was quite right to point out that Adam's inability to see any solution to his plight was no reason for his joining Eve in sin.[9] God had previously shown by creating Eve in the first place that the loneliness which Adam dreaded was something for which he

9 *Preface to Paradise Lost*, p. 123.

168

would provide. But the important thing is that Adam has a remedy and Milton of all people must know it. The remedy is divorce.

God, in instituting marriage, had not, on Milton's view, made it indissoluble. Adam's speech in Genesis of a man cleaving unto his wife and of their being one flesh stresses the strength and firmness of the marriage tie, and Milton's God, instructing Eve at her waking by the pool, makes the same point:

> hee
> Whose image thou art, him thou shalt enjoy
> Inseparablie thine . . .
>
> (IV, 471-473)

God's calling Eve 'inseparablie' Adam's involves no abandonment on Milton's part of his ideas about divorce. Milton uses the word advisedly because he is thinking of what Christ had said about Mosaic divorce: '8 He saith unto them, Moses because of the hardness of your hearts suffered you to put away your wives: but from the beginning it was not so' (St Matthew 19). So in the Garden God creates Adam and Eve 'in the beginning' as inseparably each other's, but Milton understood the words as said with reservations: 'But from the beginning it was not so . . . In the beginning, had men continud' perfet, it had bin just that all things should have remain'd as they began to *Adam & Eve* . . . Although we are not to seek, that the institution it selfe from the first beginning was never but conditional, as all cov'nants are: because thus and thus, therefore so and so; if not thus, then not so' (*Tetrachordon*, IV, 169 . . . 170 . . . 171). 'Inseparablie' has of course an additional force when it is said to Eve since it enables Milton to look forward at the same time to the fact that it was her separation from Adam that brought about her downfall. God's words to Adam about marriage however, after Adam has asked for a companion in his loneliness, say nothing about inseparability and indicate what reservations are made about the union of man and woman:

I, ere thou spak'st,
Knew it not good for Man to be alone,
And no such companie as then thou saw'st
Intended thee, for trial onely brought,
To see how thou could'st judge of fit and meet:
What next I bring shall please thee, be assur'd,
Thy likeness, thy fit help, thy other self,
Thy wish exactly to thy hearts desire.

(VIII, 444-451)

Marriage involves the judgment of what is fit and meet, and this is the sort of judgment that Adam fails to bring to bear upon the relationship when he resolves to sin with Eve. What he should do is to leave her. He would have good grounds for divorce. Eve, being Godless, is technically an unbeliever, and St Paul had spoken of marriage in such circumstances as bondage: 'But if the unbelieving depart, let him depart. A brother or a sister is not under bondage in such cases: but God hath called us to peace' (I Corinthians 7: 15), a departure which Martin Bucer interprets as being a separation from the spirit of true marriage: 'But some will say, that this is spok'n of a misbeleever departing. But I beseech yee, doth not he reject the faith of Christ in his deeds, who rashly breaks the holy covnant of wedlock instituted by God?' (*The Judgement of Martin Bucer*, IV, 53). Eve, sinful and tempting her husband to sin, has on this view departed from the covenant. Seeking to destroy her husband, she is no longer a helpmeet.

The close of Adam's fall thus provided Milton with a nice model of a divorce case. The issue of divorce was not made explicit for the simple reason that Adam and Eve were not divorced, but their final touching reconciliation in Book X is not an argument against divorce since Adam and Eve were a special case, specially assisted and hence able to make a new start. The divorce solution offered a means of pointing up the theme about God's providence which had provided Adam with his remedy, and also a means for the propagation of Milton's own thinking. So in Adam's speech it is necessary to catch not merely the devotion of the romantic lover but also the grim undertones of a poet who had made the divorce question especially his own. Milton had written too much about this sort of thing for him not to look very sarcastically at the assertion which Adam makes at the end of his speech: 'from they State/Mine never shall be parted, bliss or woe' (IX, 915–916). Adam is made to speak as though he is observing that devotion 'for better or worse' which belongs to Christian marriage, but Milton had in his prose been much concerned to define that point at which the intolerable was reached. Reconciliation was not always best. He argues in the *Christian Doctrine* that a husband who dismisses a wife who has ceased to be a helpmeet is not guilty of hardness of heart. Rather the reverse: 'Why should we think that we are displeasing God by divorcing such a one? I should attribute hardness of heart rather to him who retained her, than to him who sent her away under such circumstances' (XV, 163), and he constructs precisely the same sort of situation in *Samson*. His argument there is that a domestic tiff is not grounds for divorce, but that an offence against the whole nature of marriage, e.g. a wife's conspiring against her husband, is:

> *Chor.* Yet beauty, though injurious, hath strange power,
> After offence returning, to regain
> Love, once possest, nor can be easily
> Repuls't, without much inward passion felt
> And secret sting of amorous remorse.
> *Sam.* Love-quarrels oft in pleasing concord end,
> Not wedlock-trechery endangering life.
> (*Samson*, 1003-1009)

Here, as in *Paradise Lost*, Milton has drawn up a divorce mode whose nature he had argued extensively in his prose.

## IV

Divorce involved freedom, and a society that did not permit it was a society of compulsion, chaining an ill-matched pair to endless misery. Milton's nameless opponent in *Colasterion* had indeed argued, since St Paul had said that the married 'shall have trouble in the flesh' (I Corinthians 7: 28), that such domestic troubles were part of the inescapable unhappiness of Man's earthly lot. Milton's answer to this had been a typical plea for liberty and the responsibility of decision:

> I Answer, if this bee a true consequence, why are not all troubles to bee born alike? why are wee suffer'd to divorce adulteries, desertions, or frigidities? Who knows not that trouble and affliction is the decree of God upon every state of life? follows it therefore, that though they grow excessive, and insupportable, wee must not avoid them? if wee may in all other conditions, and not in mariage, the doom of our suffering ties us not by the trouble, but by the bond of mariage;
>
> (IV, 246-247)

On this question the idea of compulsion was as much a part of his thinking as the idea of remedy, and this comes usefully to hand in the way in which he develops Adam's fall.

Like Eve, Adam is made to step out of his Christian frame. Seeing his marriage as the indissoluble and inescapable thing, Adam makes his tragedy a satanic tragedy of necessity so that *Paradise Lost* again exemplifies the epic that belongs to the fallen, unredeemed world. The ideological context in which Adam reads himself and his situation becomes that of Hell. His last speech shows the shift, fully into the wrong:

> But past who can recall, or don undoe?
> Not God Omnipotent, nor Fate, yet so
> Perhaps thou shalt not Die . . .
> However I with thee have fixt my Lot,
> Certain to undergoe like doom, if Death
> Consort with thee, Death is to mee as Life;
> So forcible within my heart I feel
> The Bond of Nature draw me to my owne,
> My own in thee, for what thou art is mine;
> Our State cannot be severd, we are one,
> One Flesh; to loose thee were to loose my self.
>
> (IX, 926 . . . 952-959)

'Fate' is not a power for Adam to alternate so with God. 'Lot'
is here used not of something properly and reasonably ordained
by God, but as something inescapable to which Adam is
irrevocably committed. 'Doom' is no longer God's judgment;
its use here is satanic in that it is the enemy of free enterprise
as in the devils' 'doom of Battel' (II, 550). Adam is made to
speak like an heroic figure in a trap. What he called earlier the
'Link of Nature' (IX, 914) has now become the 'Bond of
Nature': 'Bond' like 'lot' and 'doom' can have either the right
or the wrong implications, but it is the wrong that are intended
here since Adam's usage is the same as Milton's own in the
quotation above from *Colasterion*, emphasizing the situation
without freedom. And whereas Adam had earlier said that he
did not want a divorce: 'And from thy State/Mine never shall
be parted, bliss or woe' (IX, 915-916), he now says that
marriage is indissoluble anyway: 'Our State cannot be severd,
we are one' (IX, 958). He chooses unfitly and unmeetly (cf.
VIII, 448) a wife who brings not solace but death, an error
grimly underlined by the punning 'Consort.' And Adam's
'Nature,' like his 'Lot,' is not something ordained by God but
is something binding and compulsive for 'what men do by
nature they do of necessity; what they do after planning they do
freely' (*Art of Logic*, XI, 41).

Adam thus sees himself as in the satanic situation of no
escape. His acceptance of this is also in the satanic mode:

> So having said, as one from sad dismay
> Recomforted, and after thoughts disturbd
> Submitting to what seemed remediless,
> Thus in calm mood his Words to *Eve* he turnd.
> (IX, 917-920)

His speech had indeed shown a fine taste in desperate gloom
and was splendidly Byronic: 'But past who can recall, or don
undoe?/Not God Omnipotent, nor Fate' (IX, 926-927), but the
tone is endorsed at risk. Adam, for all his resigned heroic tone,
is striking an attitude that Milton has characterized before. Not

173

without 'charm' it represents nevertheless the satanic way of the
'wisdom' of Hell:

> Yet with a pleasing sorcerie could charm
> Pain for a while or anguish, and excite
> Fallacious hope, or arm th'obdured brest
> With stubborn patience as with triple steel.
> (II, 566-569)

Adam's 'calm mood' is the satanic patience, stubborn because
it is hardened against all sense and against all good. It is the
apathy of the pagan stoic, not the true Christian resignation.

The bond of nature thus plays the same role in the fall of
Adam (although it has a lot more theory behind it) that hunger
plays in the fall of Eve. Adam's fall is also marked by the
same degeneration of appetite: rational sexuality becomes
irrational lust just as hunger became gluttony: 'in Lust they
burne:/Till *Adam* thus 'gan *Eve* to dalliance move' (IX, 1015-
1016). Their earlier 'dalliance' had been such as had beseemed
a 'Fair couple, linkt in happie nuptual League' (IV, 339) since
it was part of a marriage based upon reason and comfort. But
their subjection now to senses inflamed with ardour and selfish
pleasure is the satanic 'dalliance,' the lust of Satan and Sin
(II, 819). It is satanic sexuality, compulsive and irrational, as are
satanic hunger and the satanic bond of nature. It is something
that belongs naturally enough also to Dalila:

> Here I should still enjoy thee day and night
> Mine and Loves prisoner, not the *Philistines*,
> Whole to myself, unhazarded abroad,
> Fearless at hom of partners in my love.
> These reasons in Loves law have passed for good,
> Though fond and reasonless to some perhaps . . .
> (*Samson*, 807-812)

This law, devoid of respect, is no law. This, Milton argues, is
what is left of love when nothing yokes a man and a woman
but sexual appetite, or when the institution of marriage is
justified by nothing but the bond of nature. The presentation

of the Fall in terms of sexual degeneration got Milton usefully close to Genesis which seems to indicate that the ironical opening of Adam and Eve's eyes at the Fall, their new knowledge of good and evil, has to do with their nakedness, with their bodies and a sense of physical shame. But Milton fully endorsed the idea that this was indeed what the bond of nature, without reason, was reduced to. His prose indicates extensively what we are meant to see in the love-making after the Fall:

> That the ordinance which God gave to our comfort, may not be pinn'd upon us to our underserved thraldom; to be coopt up as it were in mockery of wedlock, to a perpetual betrothed lonelines and discontent if, nothing worse ensue. There being nought els of marriage left between such, but a displeasing and forc't remedy against the sting of a bruit desire: which fleshly accustoming without the souls union and commixture of intellectuall delight, as it is rather a soiling then a fulfilling of mariage-rites, so is it anough to imbase the mettle of a generous spirit, and sinks him to a low and vulgar pitch of endeavour in all his actions, or, which is wors, leavs him in a dispairing plight of abject & hard'n'd thoughts . . .
> *(Doctrine and Discipline, III, Part II, 492)*

> When love findes it self utterly unmatcht, and justly vanishes, nay rather cannot but vanish, the fleshly act indeed may continue, but not holy, not pure, not beseeming the sacred bond of mariage; beeing at best but an animal excretion, but more truly wors and more ignoble then that mute kindlyness among the heards and flocks: in that proceeding as it ought from intellective principles, it participates of nothing rational, but that which the feild and the fould equalls. For in human actions the soule is the agent, the body in a manner passive. If then the body doe out of sensitive force, what the soul complies not with, how can man, and not rather something beneath man be thought the doer.
> *(Tetrachordon, IV, 101-102)*

And what better testimony than the words of the institution it self, to prove, that a conversing solace, & peacefull society is the prime end of mariage, without which no other help, or

office can bee mutual, beseeming the dignity of reasonable
creatures, that such as they should be coupl'd in the rites of
nature by the meer compulsion of lust, without love, or peace,
wors then wild beasts.

*(Colasterion,* IV, 253)

The prose shows that Milton in no way regards Adam and
Eve's lust for each other as a misrepresentation of the case.
To him the nature of Adam's new commitment to Eve and this
final scene are inextricably connected. The understanding and
the free will, marks of Man's dignity, are both now in subjection

> To sensual Appetite, who from beneathe
> Usurping over sovran Reason claimd
> Superior sway . . .
>
> (IX, 1129-1131)

The drama of the created kinds now shows Man not promoted
to Angel but reduced to Animal, and the drama of literary
kinds shows Man the hero not of the Christian but of the
satanic poem.

Milton's poem about Adam's case reflects his temperament.
Wilful disregard of duties and law is anarchic. The recriminations which Adam and Eve direct at each other at the end of
Book IX are, on Milton's view, not accidental but the logical
outcome of their lawlessness. Living without law, they live
without security and guarantee. Their quarrel at the end is
characteristic of their acquired unreliability. If Eve does not
take Adam's advice that she should not garden on her own, if
Adam does not insist on his proper authority with her, if she
does establish an irrational relationship—all of which things
Book IX has been about—then there is nothing to safeguard
them from the bitterness and change of temper at the end of the
Book. Milton's preference is for the life lived according to
order and reason and a just and specific set of rules. Self-
awareness, a clear sense of what is proper and reasonable in any
relationship or duty, are the marks of the reasonable and just

man. His view of life carried with it a sense of vocation and purpose. Samson too has this: he was a Nazarite, and the self-conscious deliverer of his people. Milton himself was called to all sorts of vocations, to be the poet, the defender of liberty. Without seeing the importance of this complex of objectives and rights within which the good life is ordered, we cannot understand the life of Milton's Garden, or the true nature of Adam's fall. The latter marked a failure of responsibility. The virtue of Adam and Eve was never, like Satan's momentary lapse into goodness (IX, 465), stupid, nor was Adam the 'meer artificiall *Adam*, such an *Adam* as he is in the motions' (*Areopagitica*, IV, 319) although that is what Milton designedly made him at his fall. The innocence of Adam and Eve had always been adult, their marriage a vocation, and their responsibility a call to obey, Eve to obey her husband, Adam to obey God. The Lady of *Comus* is also typical with her intelligent and argumentative virtue. Comus's victims were the incautious and the ignorant (*Comus*, 537). The life of the good is lived under moral strain. Milton's account of the Fall is thus a deeply human and moral episode. The mythological aspects of *Paradise Lost* must not be allowed to obscure the real nature of Milton's achievement. Satan's role for example is practically superseded once the human centre of the poem is established. Satan has nothing to do with the real responsibility for Eve's fall, nor with Adam's own sin, and Milton has no need of him in the rest of the poem when it is concerned with human life after the Fall and its sequence of sin and error. Guilt and folly have human images.

# 9

# The Aftermath

## I

ALTHOUGH God's providence was just as much asserted by what came after the Fall as by what went before it so that the thesis of *Paradise Lost* was in no way superseded after Book IX, nevertheless the 'disposition' of the poem offered some difficulty after that point. Until the end of Book IX it had been very much a poem of the clenched fist. Its episodes for all their variety had all pressed hard around one central point, and a lot of subtle thinking and organization had been required in order to tease rationality out of the Genesis account of the Fall. But after Book IX the logical pressure of the poem was less intense. In seeing the workings of God's providence in what happened after the Fall, Milton was putting a familiar and easier case. There was still room for some exercise of logic and invention. Genesis does not say, for example, that Adam and Eve were reconciled nor that Eve suggested suicide as a possible remedy for their distress. This lack of an immediate aftermath of the Fall needed to be filled by commentary. Calvin takes the fact that Adam and Eve eventually had children to imply that they had been saved from despair: on his view God had made the prophecy about Eve's seed bruising the serpent's head (Genesis 3: 15) in order to confirm their hearts.[1] Milton, in Book X, 1028-1096, makes the same point. This assumption that Adam and Eve's despair was relieved gave him warrant for other episodes, the visit of Michael for instance which was also intended to exhort and reassure. But the poem necessarily became less deductive and controversial, its thesis less open to challenge or satanic misreadings. Though its main argument stood, it was less easy to provide interesting and unusual demonstration of it. Nor, since the poem has to cover so much ground, do the episodes allow of so much expansion in the way of emotional variety and human interest.

Book XII most obviously shows the problem. Its main line, Biblical history seen in terms of God's providence, leaves little enough room for original interpretation at the best of times, and here, given the proportions of the poem, no time at all. The poem proceeds unusually by compression and selection, a very different manner of working from that which had been required before and at the Fall. Milton cannot leave out too much, otherwise the continuity of the thesis would not be apparent. So he is forced into a very cursory manner of writing. He opens the book with some further development of his thesis about individual responsibility, relating the establishment of political tyranny to the moral failure of the individual, loss of reason being punished by loss of liberty (XII, 79-96). He thus usefully gets his thesis on to a political line which, given his own interests and experience, is important to him. But his treatment has, most uncharacteristically, to be uncontroversial and unquarrelsome since he has no scope for expansion. The political line has to be quickly abandoned so as not to obscure the main theme concerned with the election of the Jewish people and the promise of Messiah. The same point holds with regard to the issue of clerical authority and discipline. This is again too familiar a cause of dispute for Milton to let it go by without a fight, but the most that the proportions of the book permit is a breathless incursion into

[1] *Institutes* (Book II, ch. xiii), trans. Beveridge, I, 412.

invective (XII, 507-539). This is very different from the case at the Fall where the story can be fully centred on the issues of marriage and divorce and developed at length and relevantly in respect to them. Furthermore the inventions that any one particular episode in Book XII might have allowed were forbidden by the scale of the Book. If, for example, Samson had been included as a type of Christian hero, there would have been little room for Dalila, even less (if any at all) for Manoa, and none at all for Harapha who, being a fiction and not a logically necessary one, could not have been permitted into what was now a history. And the climax of Book XII, the Incarnation, is not reached with any notable growth or development. The promises about Messiah are not disposed in any significant order, nor do the types of Christ get bigger and better types. As a drama, Christian history has a beginning and an end, but no middle. Like the account of the war in Heaven in Book VI, Book XII offers for the most part less logical challenge and opportunity, and the lacklustre response which is all that it arouses in most of its readers shows how important are the logic and tautness of the poem elsewhere.

II

But the account of what happened after the Fall gave Milton room for originality in one important respect. The Fall had been seen not merely in terms of the logic of the poem's thesis but also in terms of the logic of its literary kind. The 'argument' had provided the occasion for a literary contention. This contention can still be made to go on after the Fall, and as it is an issue with which ordinary Biblical commentary was not at all concerned, Milton won for himself some room to work and some freedom of interpretation.

Book IX had dramatized an issue of literary theory: the Christian and satanic modes of tragedy and epic had been juxtaposed and discriminated. The Fall, seen in the proper way, is a model Christian tragedy: God is providential, and poetical justice is established.[2] Furthermore, besides being tragic in itself, it also made all other tragedy possible since its outcome brought sin and death into the world. Adam and Eve look to a tragic future. It was one ordained for them by God:

17 . . . cursed is the ground for thy sake; in sorrow shalt thou eat of it all the days of thy life;

18 Thorns also and thistles shall it bring forth to thee; and thou shalt eat the herb of the field;

19 In the sweat of thy face shalt thou eat bread, till thou return unto the ground; for out of it wast thou taken: for dust thou art, and unto dust shalt thou return.

(Genesis 3)

and the implications of these verses allowed of some extension in the poem.

The tragic life of Man thus ordained by God concerned not merely Adam and Eve but also their descendants, and just as he had demonstrated that Adam and Eve's tragedy was not one of bad luck or necessity, so Milton looks carefully to the implications of the other tragedies that are to follow. Thus Adam, talking to Eve, surveys the sadness of Man's life that is to come:

Since this days Death denounc't, if ought I see,
Will prove no sudden, but a slow-pac't evill,
A long days dying to augment our paine,
And to our Seed (O hapless Seed!) deriv'd.
    To whom thus *Eve*, recovering heart, repli'd.
*Adam*, by sad experiment I know
How little weight my words with thee can finde,

[2] Northrop Frye, *Anatomy of Criticism* (Princeton, 1957), pp. 211-213 sees *Paradise Lost* as expounding the archetypal myth of tragedy. Adam's fall represents his entering the order of nature, a narrowing of freedom into the law. Frye of course is more concerned to see it as representing his own theory of the tragic mode which is 'the symbolic presentation of the point at which the undisplaced apocalyptic world and the cyclical world of nature come into alignment' (p. 203) and which 'seems to elude the antithesis of moral responsibility and arbitrary fate, just as it eludes the antithesis of good and evil' (p. 211). Milton's interest in the poem, as I read it, is of course very much with these antitheses, but far from eluding them I think that he is very anxious to point up one set and play down the other.

Found so erroneous, thence by just event
Found so unfortunate . . .
If care of our descent perplex us most,
Which must be born to certain woe, devourd
By Death at last . . .
It lies, yet ere Conception to prevent
The Race unblest, to being yet unbegot.

(X, 962 . . . 979 . . . 987-988)

This contains some key words that show Milton's alert reading of the situation. Adam and Eve are made to be concerned about the ideology of the tragedy in which they and their seed are involved. Adam's 'hapless' shows that he sees his descendants as subject to bad luck. Eve, taking up this point, shows that she has learned to read their particular situation rightly. Their own misery is not undeserved: it is a 'just event,' showing the proper distribution of punishment. But Eve too looks feelingly to the misery of those yet to be born. She firstly, like Adam, reads it as bad luck ('unfortunate'), but secondly as a necessity, a 'certain' woe. Thus in this way, the inescapable nature of God's doom, the fact that Adam's sin is the original sin which infects all his descendants, could be taken as a satanic tragedy of inescapable suffering. Milton is anxious to avoid this. The innate depravity of Man was something that he was never much concerned to stress in his writings since it worked against the moral freedom he always upheld. So in the poem Adam's reassurance to Eve after this speech, and Michael's later reassurances to him are intended to show that Man's lot is no satanic case: things are not all that gloomy and not at all hopeless.

But the sin of Adam and Eve has for the first time made satanic tragedy possible. Doom and mischance are become part of Man's life. From this time on, for example, Man lives in a violent and predatory animal world since he has lost his dominion over the beasts (X, 707-714). Milton himself will not read these tragedies in a satanic way (since the good are rewarded in Heaven), but those writers who do now have material to hand for the first time. The Fall made possible a world of the victimization of Man.

This is what Book X is much concerned with. Just as Adam's sin was the prototype of the sin of Man, so the Garden is now the prototype of the tragic scene. One of the most marked exemplifications of the new regimen under which Man now lives is the new role of the sky in human affairs. Over the uncorrupted Garden the stars had shed 'sweet influence' (VII, 375), but with the Fall their aspect is changed:

> To the blanc Moone
> Her office they prescrib'd, to th'other five
> Thir planetarie motions and aspects
> In *Sextile*, *Square*, and *Trine*, and *Opposite*,
> Of noxious efficacie, and when to joyne
> In synod unbenigne, and taught the fixt
> Thir influence malignant when to showre,
> Which of them rising with the Sun, or falling,
> Should prove tempestuous . . .
> (X, 656-664)

Here is the origin of what, to many writers, constituted the tragic case. Caesar's tragedy was for example played out under an ominous and malignant sky:

> As stars with trains of fire and dews of blood,
> Disasters in the sun; and the moist star
> Upon whose influence Neptune's empire stands
> Was sick almost to doomsday with eclipse.
> (*Hamlet*, I, i, 117-120)

and Othello (wrongly) attributes his misfortune to the 'error of the moon' which strikes the Earth with madness (*Othello*, V, ii, 109). Milton's own deliberate constructions in *Lycidas* of pagan tragic patterns within which to see King's death had ended in recourse to the inauspicious heavens:

> It was that fatall and perfidious Bark
> Built in th'eclipse, and rigg'd with curses dark,
> That sunk so low that sacred head of thine . . .
> (*Lycidas*, 100-102)

183

The world of the stars, typifying the world of the inescapable threat, was very much part of the world of satanic tragedy of mischance and doom. Milton's development of this model in Book X has an especial advantage. It is a model of satanic tragedy, but in this one unique case it was subject to and consequent upon, not prior to and responsible for Man's plight. It is effect not cause. It is thus put in the right framework of justice and law and reason. There is no randomness in this change of the sky since it is ordained by God, Milton making a logical extrapolation from the curse on life on Earth in Genesis. The model is one of order, the change in the Heavens moves by law and precept: the sun 'Had first his precept so to move, so shine' (X, 652); so also for the moon 'Her office they prescrib'd' (X, 657). The stars are 'taught' (X, 661) their new motions, and the corners of the winds are 'set' (X, 664). The impression is importantly one of control.

Although the curse on the Earth is related in Genesis, it was St Paul who had first and impressively sounded the theme of the full defilement of Nature as well as of Man at the Fall:

> 21 Because the creature itself also shall be delivered from the bondage of corruption into the glorious liberty of the children of God.
> 22 For we know that the whole creation groaneth and travaileth in pain together until now. (Romans 8)[3]

St Paul, it can be seen, looks at the theme not at all satanically since he knows that the children of God can be freed from corruption. The acceptance of his view held some interesting problems. For Genesis gives not only God's curse upon the ground at the Fall but also what appears to be the removal of that curse at the Flood:

> 21 . . . and the LORD said in his heart, I will not again curse the ground any more for man's sake; for the imagination of man's heart is evil from his youth; neither will I again smite any more every thing living, as I have done.

[3] See N. P. Williams, *The Ideas of the Fall and of Original Sin* (London, 1927), esp. pp. 157-159

22 While the earth remaineth, seedtime and harvest, and cold and heat, and summer and winter, and day and night shall not cease.

(Genesis 8)

This makes it seem that Nature no longer partakes of corruption, which belongs only to Man, in which case St Paul is wrong. Milton, familiar with the literary reverberations of the Pauline theme, prefers to follow Paul. Hence his own account of the Flood omits any reference to the removal of the curse on the ground, God merely setting up his covenant not to destroy the Earth again:

> his Cov'nant: Day and Night,
> Seed time and Harvest, Heat and hoary Frost
> Shall hold thir course, till fire purge all things new,
> Both Heav'n and Earth, wherein the just shall dwell.

(XI, 898-901)

Milton did not suppose that the tragic theme of general woe had been superannuated at the Flood.

The satanic model itself is thus in Book X made to provide an example of the proper poetical justice. This connection of the results of Adam's sin and literary tragedy is not peculiar to Milton. Calvin is also explicit about it. According to his reading, Moses does not mention all the disadvantages of Adam's sin, those of cold, frost, storm and disease. Calvin is, like Milton, following Paul rather than Genesis, assuming that there were other tribulations visited upon Man as a result of his sin than those included in the curse on the ground, so that even if the latter were removed, the others remained. Man's suffering is not simply confined to the difficulty of getting crops out of the earth. Calvin supports this Pauline view by reference to its echoes in literature: 'This has been celebrated in poetical fables, and was doubtless handed down, by tradition, from the Fathers,'[4] and establishes his point with a quotation from Horace (*Odes*, III, iii). Milton's advantage is that his

---

[4] *Commentaries upon Genesis*, trans. King, I, 177.

treatment of the issue in poetry rather than commentary enabled him to exploit it more extensively and subtly.

So Adam first and most properly might sound that note of general lament, of mutability and transience, that echoes down after him among the poets:

> To the loss of that,
> Sufficient penaltie, why hast thou added
> The sense of endless woes? (X, 752-754)

This is the first 'complaint.' The Fall not merely brought about Death, but also sentiments about Death and about the insecurity of life. It made possible a whole convention of writing:

> O trustlesse state of earthly things, and slipper hope
> Of mortal men, that swincke and sweat for nought,
> And shooting wide, doe misse the marked scope:
> Now have I learnd (a lesson derely bought)
> That nys on earth assurance to be sought . . .
> (Spenser, *Shepheardes Calendar*, *November*
> *Eclogue*, l.153-157)

This theme of general woe has a relevance at this point in *Paradise Lost* where it is permitted within a system. It is not a feeling which Milton indulged in the rest of his work and forms no part of his own elegiac writing. It is, for instance, interestingly absent from *Lycidas* where Milton does not argue that the death of King is merely the particular example of a general process of mutability, part of a doom that belongs to all terrestrial Nature. Only at one point does *Lycidas* appear to be saying that Nature is transitory and thus tragically committed:

> As killing as the Canker to the Rose,
> Or Taint-worm to the weanling Herds that graze,
> Or Frost to Flowers, that their gay wardrop wear,
> When first the White thorn blows;
> Such, *Lycidas*, thy loss to Shepherds ear.
> (*Lycidas*. 45-49)

but the logic of this connects the *news* of Lycidas's death and not that death itself with the general process: the canker kills the rose, the worm the herds, the frost the flowers, as the *tidings* of the death has affected the shepherd's ear. The only generalization that Milton uses in *Lycidas* is that of King, not as a tragic type of humanity in general, but as a type of certain classes of men, of the dedicated poets and the conscientious pastors. Milton's mind was very resistant to the lack of discrimination that the over-all tragic view of things usually involved. The third chorus of Samson (652-704) runs off what seems a gloomy tragic pattern, but it is characteristically concerned with a particular type of situation: the chorus is perplexed by a world that seems to involve no poetical justice. Samson's suffering seems disproportionate and unjust, and this prompts the chorus to make some damaging inferences about the way in which the world is governed. The issue is still not one of universal suffering but only that of the guilty who nevertheless seem over-harshly beset. Milton of course entertained no illusions about Man's earthly lot: 'Generally speaking, however, no distinction is made between the righteous and the wicked, with regard to the final issue of events, at least in this life' (*Christian Doctrine*, XV, 61). Man was 'born to trouble as the sparks fly upward' (Job 5: 7). But true poetry was concerned with the heavenly dimension of justice and reason. He preferred also to wrestle with the individual case. The complaint of universal tragic woe can be included in Book X of *Paradise Lost* because it was meaningful with respect to Adam's case and because it had warrant in what God said, so Milton's use of it involved no loss of discrimination, no unprofitable blurring of the issues.

III

So Book X, in its presentation of Man's situation, contributes to the poem's demonstration about the theory of literary kinds. Tragedy is made an instituted ordained kind. This

argument proceeds in Book XI. Milton still needs to indicate
how God's providence is made manifest in the fallen world
outside the Garden, and thus to say more about the logic of the
true Christian poem. Adam, who saw himself in the wrong
scheme after his fall, must be made aware of the right scheme
and what his role in it is. The vision of the future which he is
shown by Michael is instructive in this way.[5] It also enables
Milton to make Adam experience the full awareness of his sin,
since the vision creates in him that sense of belonging to a
sinful race that his descendants have in knowing themselves o
be of his seed. In thus making Adam's view of human sinfulness as total as that of his descendants is, Milton presents an
Adam not merely archetypal but also typical. Hence Adam  i
also given access to the consolation that later ages have when
Michael, at the end of the poem, gives him the knowledge of
Man's Redemption. All this involved some shift in the part
played by Adam. He becomes not actor but spectator, instructed and brought to understanding by Michael. If this
caused some difficulty in that the poem obviously had to move
by way of presentation followed by explanation, it was also an
opportunity. If Adam had eventually to get things right, he
could be shown first to get them wrong. The episodes can thus
proceed by differentiation, by means of the right and the
wrong, the Christian and the satanic explication of plot and
situation. Book XI has thus a lot to do with literary theory.

Starting his lesson, Michael tells Adam what he is about to
relate, its matter, intention, and the proper response which
it should arouse:

> good with bad
> Expect to hear, supernal Grace contending
> With sinfulness of Men; thereby to learn
> True patience, and to temper joy with fear
> And pious sorrow, equally enur'd

[5] Summers, *The Muse's Method*, pp. 186-224 has a very good account of the last
two books of the poem. Though I point to much of the same detail that he does, I
am of course concerned to fit it into a different frame.

By moderation either state to beare,
Prosperous or adverse: so shalt thou lead
Safest thy life, and best prepar'd endure
Thy mortal passage when it comes.
(XI, 358-366)

'True patience,' 'fear,' 'pious sorrow' (catharsis, fear and pity
in more usual literary-critical terms) show that Milton's
concern in the episode is with tragedy. The patience that
Michael recommends is based on St Paul:

8 We are troubled on every side, yet not distressed; we are
perplexed, but not in despair . . .

17 For our light affliction, which is but for a moment, worketh
for us a far more exceeding and eternal weight of glory;
18 While we look not at the things which are seen, but at the
things which are not seen: for the things which are seen are
temporal; but the things which are not seen are eternal.
(II Corinthians 4)

9 Now I rejoice, not that ye were made sorry, but that ye
sorrowed to repentance: for ye were made sorry after a godly
manner, that ye might receive damage by us in nothing.

10 For godly sorrow worketh repentance to salvation not to be
repented of: but the sorrow of the world worketh death.
(II Corinthians 7)

and the point of his visit is to expose Adam to this sorrow of
the world which indeed for the first time works death. St
Paul thus provides Milton with his definition of the right sort
of catharsis, patience of the right kind, looking to the heavenly
dimension ('the things which are not seen'), not of the wrong
satanic kind, as exemplified in the songs of Hell (II, 569) and
in Adam's 'calm mood' (IX, 920) after his fall. This discrimination about patience was common enough. Calvin says,
characterizing the Stoic apathy as 'a shadow of patience,'[6] that
the Christian can bear prosperity or adversity with equanimity

---

[6] *Institutes* (Book III, ch. viii), trans. Beveridge, II, 21.

because 'his affairs are ordered by the Lord in the manner most conducive to his salvation.'[7] Milton's skill is again shown in the manipulation of the moral commonplace in terms of the true and false poem. In confronting Adam with a set of tragedies and so providing what looks like a blank verse version of the *Trinity MS.*, Milton's concern is to see the tragic facts in the light of the proper metaphysical and moral implications. The response to them needs to be intellectual as well as emotional, and the emotions that they arouse need to be justified. More even than being moved, Adam must come to understand.

Michael begins by showing to Adam the world's first tragedy of physical death, the murder of Abel. It is the spectacle of the just man as victim and, faced with this plot, Adam and Michael see different implications in it. Seeing it in terms of the earthly dimension, Adam sees it as unjust and mysterious: 'Is Pietie thus and pure Devotion paid?' (XI, 452) but Michael, though moved, sees it in relation to a just and rational heavenly scheme:

> the bloodie Fact
> Will be aveng'd, and th'others Faith approv'd
> Loose no reward, though here thou see him die,
> Rowling in dust and gore.
>
> (XI, 457-460)

Cain's vice will be punished, Abel's virtue rewarded. Adam is given his first lesson in divine and hence poetical justice.

In this death of Abel, Adam has witnessed death by violence, and the poem is now concerned to establish the right prototype of Death in the world. Adam did not indeed at first know that what he had seen was death, calling it merely 'some great mischief' (XI, 450). Instructed in its true name, Adam then proceeds to see that particular death as the tragic prototype: what the forbidden Fruit had brought into the world was that particular sort of violent end:

[7] ibid. (Book III, ch. vii), II, 14.

> Is this the way
> I must return to native dust? O sight
> Of terrour, foul and ugly to behold,
> Horrid to think, how horrible to feel!
> (XI, 462-465)

Adam's response, terror and horror, is proper to the tragic
case, but Adam has generalized the episode all the wrong way.
Death has, as Michael points out, many forms:

> many are the wayes that lead
> To his grim Cave, all dismal; yet to sense
> More terrible at th'entrance then within.
> (XI, 468-470)

Properly tragic ('dismal, 'terrible'), the case, even in the earthly
dimension, needs to be more carefully discriminated: Death is
less grim than dying. But what Michael goes on to show Adam,
the hospital scene with its ghastly series of malady and pain, is
in all truth grim enough. What is stressed here in Adam's
response is not horror but pity, Aristotle as well as St Paul
sharpening Milton's sense of the issues:

> compassion quell'd
> His best of Man, and gave him up to tears
> A space, till firmer thoughts restraind excess,
> And scarce recovering words his plaint renew'd.
> (496-499)

That firmer thoughts discipline what might be mere indulgence
in sentiment is creditable, except that Adam goes on to make
all the wrong deductions from the facts before him:

> why should not Man,
> Retaining still Divine similitude
> In part, from such deformities be free,
> And for his Makers Image sake exempt?
> (XI, 511-514)

But Adam's question, as Michael sees it, is not a sensible one,
being rooted merely in feeling. Michael, diagnosing these
chronic diseases as being the result of intemperance, reads the

scene as a tragedy brought about by human failure of responsibility and self-control. It sounds a brutal diagnosis but it is
one that Milton offers in all sincerity:[8] *Samson* also presents
these sorts of disease as 'the punishment of dissolute days'
(702) though it allows, as the poem here does not, that some
who have not been disordinate in their lives are still nevertheless sometimes afflicted with such diseases in their old age
(698-702). But Milton reads such tragedies here as just ones,
and the scene becomes an especially useful model since,
showing as it thus does the tragedy of ungoverned appetite, it
can be made to look back to the fall of Eve. It plays out the
same thesis, that the perversion of nature's rules degrades.
But Man is now not only actor—perpetrator and sufferer—of
the deed; he is also spectator and critic. Adam recognizes, as
Eve in Book IX did not, that such a tragic scene poses no
mysterious and unanswerable question but shows justly the
punishment of the wicked: 'I yield it just, said *Adam*, and
submit' (XI, 526).

But Adam is still anxious to establish his true model of
Death:

> But is there yet no other way, besides
> These painful passages, how we may come
> To Death, and mix with our connatural dust?
>
> (XI, 527-529)

So, having seen murder and the agony of chronic illness, what
arises out of mischance and out of human intemperance, he is
shown what will happen if he lives, unmurdered and moderate.
But Michael's picture of ripened age is not an apparently
reassuring one:

> in thy blood will reigne
> A melancholy damp of cold and dry
> To weigh thy Spirits down, and last consume
> The Balme of Life.
>
> (XI, 543-545)

[8] See Svendsen, *Milton and Science*, p. 203.

This final scene is different from the others in that the death it shows is like the dropping of ripe fruit rather than a violent wresting away from life, but, being still tragic, it forces Adam to be open-eyed and unillusioned about his situation. There is no complacency in Michael's picture: the Fall represented the introduction of tragedy into human experience, and this particular scene is the common human lot. Age, if one has the good luck and the good judgment to survive that long, is inescapable. Shocked by the spectacle, Adam again makes the wrong deduction from it. He sees Death as a good, but that is to surrender wholly to the feelings without referring them back to the standard of what is just and reasonable. Michael's flat rebuke puts Adam's emotions in their place:

> Nor love thy Life, nor hate; but what thou livst
> Live well, how long or short permit to Heav'n . . .
> (XI, 553-554)

Adam has now been shown Death in all its modes. Instructed in its nature, he has also been led to survey it with appropriate emotions.

He has been presented in particular with a true picture of the tragedy of appetite that constituted Eve's fall, and he is next instructed in the tragedy of 'nature' which constituted his own.[9] Michael, showing him the corruption of the just men by the bevy of fair women (XI, 556-637), presents the episode as one about marriage whose only union is sensual pleasure and the bond of nature:

> And now of love they treat till th'Eevning Star
> Loves Harbinger appeerd; then all in heat
> They light the Nuptial Torch, and bid invoke
> Hymen, then first to marriage Rites invok't;

[9] Williams, *The Common Expositor*, p. 152 states that the commentators stressed the extensive effects of these marriages (see XI, 683-697), but Milton's point is to make them part of his thesis about the Fall and marriage itself. Michael Fixler, *Milton and the Kingdoms of God* (London, 1964), pp. 230-231 sees this phase of history as dominated by the sin of uxuriousness and reflecting Eve's involvement in Adam's sin. The responsibility is Adam's though on my view.

With Feast and Musick all the Tents resound.
Such happy interview and fair event
Of love and youth not lost, Songs, Garlands, Flours,
And charming Symphonies attach'd the heart
Of *Adam*, soon enclin'd to admit delight,
The bent of Nature . . .

(XI, 588-597)

The 'soft amorous Ditties' and the 'dance' (XI, 584) which serve as a prelude to this love-making show that it is satanic and corrupt, and the key word 'charming' shows the line along which Milton is working. This is marriage based not upon a reasonable institution, but upon 'heat,' 'delight,' and 'the bent of nature' only, and that 'Hymen' is invoked shows its unChristian basis. Adam's response, as it did before at the Fall, again lacks discrimination:

Much better seems this Vision, and more hope
Of peaceful dayes portends, then those two past;
Those were of hate and death, or pain much worse,
Here Nature seems fulfilld in all her ends.

(XI, 599-602)

Whereas he had in the previous scenes made an error about the implications of the tragic kind, he here makes an error about what kind the scene really is. Trust in the feelings only leads to error. Significantly, Adam's lack of judgment about this particular case leads to loss of judgment about all the others that he had previously seen. What he has seen before was not, as he now says, 'hate, and death, or pain much worse.' This is to ignore all Michael's schooling about them. Adam's hold on the good and the true is easily lost. In showing the power of even a moment's relaxation Milton is presenting an important lesson about vigilance. Herbert, also a master of this sort of thing, images the same lesson in the actual structure of his sonnet 'Sinne' ('LORD, with what care has thou begirt us round'), where the first thirteen lines, listing at length Man's defences

against sin (parents, laws, etc.), are nevertheless utterly over-
born by the one last line:

> Yet all these fences and their whole aray
> One cunning bosome-sinne blows quite away.

Man can easily be deceived about his security.
Michael again spells out the right reading for Adam:

> Judg not what is best
> By pleasure, though to Nature seeming meet,
> Created, as thou art, to nobler end
> Holie and pure, comformitie divine.
>
> (XI, 603-606)

The point that Michael makes about Adam's nature serves to
illustrate how different Milton's matter here is from his matter
before the Fall. It is simpler, needing less complication.
Discussing appetite here, he needs no recourse to angels
and their hypothetical sexuality since his aim is not to establish
the innocence of appetite but the possibility of its misuse, a
not unusual point to make. This latter Raphael had also
discussed, but he had furthermore to show that Adam's
having appetites at all was no indictment of God's providence.
Something more than the moralist was required by the poem
before the Fall, whereas its case here needs less elaborate
preparation. Michael takes of course the same view of nature
that Raphael had: the marriages that Adam is watching are
based upon unreason and hence are immoral. They will,
necessarily, since God is just, come to a tragic end:

> To these that sober Race of Men, whose lives
> Religious titl'd them the Sons of God,
> Shall yield up all thir vertue, all thir fame
> Ignobly, to the traines and to the smiles
> Of these fair Atheists, and now swim in joy,
> (Erelong to swim at large) and laugh; for which
> The world erelong a world of tears must weepe . . .
>
> (XI, 621-627)

The end of Book XI is the Flood, to which Michael's phrase 'swim in joy' points grimly forward. But it points back also to the dalliance of Adam and Eve at the Fall 'They swim in mirth' (IX, 1009). This episode about the Sons of God is thus part of the poem's thesis about marriage. (Milton has good reason therefore for insisting as he does that the phrase 'Sons of God' does not mean angels but one-time sober men.) Adam is this time *reading* the situation badly, not *playing* it himself. His first error was about the nature of the scene when it had seemed to image joy rather than woe. His next is about the responsibility for it:

> But still I see the tenor of Mans woe
> Holds on the same, from Woman to begin.
>
> (IX, 632-631)

Michael reads it differently: the fault is not Woman's but Man's:

> From Mans effeminate slackness it begins,
> Said th'Angel, who should better hold his place
> By wisedome, and superior gifts receav'd.
>
> (XI, 634-636)

This again looks back, this time to Adam's weakness in letting Eve have her own way in going off alone. Milton's intention in all this is to make the Flood relate directly to what happened at the Fall. Genesis anyway provided him a model neo-classical story here: the story of the Flood and the events leading up to it shows not merely the punishments visited upon the unjust but also the salvation of the just: Enoch is rescued from the violent hands of his enemies and transferred to Heaven (XI, 705-710) and Noah is preserved at the Flood (XI, 817-821, 890). But Milton makes his story of the Flood more than this. On the thesis that he presents, the corruption of the world that was destroyed at the Flood had its origin in a perversion of the marriage relationship, a failure in wisdom and authority, a yielding to nature. The Flood is thus treated with some originality and made a radical part of the argument of the poem.

The episodes of Book XI thus have a beautifully logical disposition. The isolated and disconnected episodes of Genesis are collated into a system that is concerned with the thesis of the poem and looks back also to the Fall.[10] The matter is managed also through Milton's organic use of literary theory, his insistence (through Michael) on the proper interpretation of the tragic and epic kinds.

## IV

Although Book XII, as argued earlier, is less interesting and original for the most part, yet the climax and close of that book are developed with some theoretical elaboration. Given Milton's concern with Christ as hero,[11] it would be surprising if he did not make his account of the Redemption contribute to the literary contention of his poem. He develops it so as to achieve a nice paradox about the tragic and the epic. Michael's account to Adam of the coming of the Messiah is in the epic mode:

> A Virgin is his Mother, but his Sire
> The Power of the most High; he shall ascend
> The Throne hereditarie, and bound his Reign
> With earths wide bounds, his glory with the Heav'ns.
>
> (XII, 368-371)

and Adam accordingly proceeds to see Christ's fight with Satan in traditional (and hence wrong) epic terms: 'say where and when/Thir fight, what stroke shall bruise the Victors heel' (XII, 384-385). But Milton has previously, at the opening of Book IX, characterized the especial role of Christ as being that of 'Patience and Heroic Martyrdom' (32), and Michael now proceeds to outline that role to Adam in what, in the earthly dimension, sound like tragic rather than epic terms:

[10] On the way in which *Paradise Regained* is also made to look back to the Fall, see Elizabeth M. Pope, *Paradise Regained: the Tradition and the Poem* (Baltimore, 1947), pp. 51-69.

[11] On Christ as hero, see Merritt Y. Hughes, 'The Christ of "Paradise Regained" and the Renaissance Heroic Tradition,' *SP*, XXXV (1938), pp. 254-277; and Kermode, 'Milton's Hero,' *RES*, n.s., IV (1953), 317-330.

thy punishment
He shall endure by coming in the Flesh
To a reproachful life and cursed death . . .
For this he shall live hated, be blasphem'd,
Seis'd on by force, judg'd, and to death condemnd
A shameful and accurst, naild to the Cross
By his own Nation, slaine for bringing Life . . .
(XII; 404 . . . 411-414)

But what, on Earth, is the tragic mode turns out, in Heaven,
to be the epic one:

so he dies,
But soon revives, Death over him no power
Shall long usurp; ere the third dawning light
Returne, the Starres of Morn shall see him rise
Out of his grave, fresh as the dawning light . . .
(XII, 419-423)

The Christian paradox of triumph through suffering and
humility is presented here characteristically sharpened by
literary theory.

The close of the poem also demonstrates a deliberate
procedure. The way in which Adam and Eve departed from
the Garden:

They hand in hand with wandring steps and slow
Through *Eden* took thir solitarie way.
(XII, 648-649)

caused some confusion amongst eighteenth-century critics
who were properly interested in the logical and literary
constraints within which the poem was operating. Addison
for example regarded the pathos of the close as failing to
provide the reader with the tranquillity and satisfaction that
belonged to the truly cathartic close:

These two Verses, though they have their Beauty, fall very
much below the foregoing Passage, and renew in the Mind of the
Reader that Anguish which was pretty well laid by that Con-
sideration:

The World was all before them, where to chuse,
Their place of rest, and Providence their Guide.[12]

Bentley of course argued the issue even more extensively ('It contradicts the Poet's own scheme')[13] to the extent of providing his own improved version. To both Addison and Bentley the ending thus lacked system and offended against the self-consistency of the poem. Pearce, stepping through detail by detail, was able to answer Bentley by pointing out that the end does square with the manner in which God had told Michael to dismiss Adam and Eve, 'So send them forth, though sorrowing, yet in peace' (XI, 117), but still failed to see fully what was conditioning Milton's manner.[14] Milton needed a very fine balance. Even before Michael comes to Adam and Eve, Milton's description of how their prayers and repentance have served to reconcile them again to God shows how, in taking away some of their sorrow, he is anxious not to give too much to their joy:

when *Adam* and first Matron *Eve*
Had ended now thir Orisons, and found
Strength added from above, new hope to spring
Out of despaire, joy, but with fear yet linkt . . .
(XI, 136-139)

Their cause for joy needs to be subtly balanced against their cause for woe so as not to let the one outweigh the other. The thesis of the Fortunate Fall cannot be allowed to cancel out the tragic element in the poem or the tragic element still possible to Man's life.[15] Adam's doubt at the end of Michael's disclosures is thus necessary:

---

[12] *Spectator*, No. 369.
[13] Ed. *Paradise Lost*, p. 399.
[14] *A Review of the Text of Paradise Lost*, p. 385-389.
[15] Arthur O. Lovejoy, 'Milton and the Paradox of the Fortunate Fall,' *ELH*, IV (1937), 161-179 makes the point that Milton wishes to keep the Fall and the Redemption very separate from each other in the poem and stresses how Adam's doubt is therefore necessary. My point is that this is an emotional as well as a theoretical feature of the close.

full of doubt I stand,
Whether I should repent me now of sin
By mee done and occasiond, or rejoyce
Much more, that much more good thereof shall spring.
(XII, 473-476)

His doubt is that of a hero with a tragic past who does not, indeed cannot, know what literary kind the end of the play is to be, but who has more occasion to be reassured (though not complacent) about his future than he is depressed about his past. Milton has to hold feelings of joy and woe together in reconcilement, knowing exactly what belongs and gives rise to each. Michael thus tells Adam that he leaves them (as God had said that he should):

Both in one Faith unanimous though sad,
With cause for evils past, yet much more cheer'd
With meditation on the happie end.
(XII, 603-605)

and the last lines of the poem thus touch the same points:

They looking back, all th'Eastern side beheld
Of Paradise, so late thir happie seat,
Wav'd over by that flaming Brand, the Gate
With dreadful Faces throng'd, and fierie Armes:
The World was all before them, where to choose
Thir place of rest, and Providence thir guide:
They hand in hand with wandring steps and slow,
Through *Eden* took thir solitarie way.
(XII, 641-648)

The mixture of regret and hope, retribution and promise is deliberate. Milton, anxious to strike the proper note, knows how ambiguous (though not confusing) his literary kind here is. His ending is perfectly consistent with a scheme that does not want at this point to commit itself fully to either joy or woe, or to one literary kind. He is thus not merely writing a touching scene, though it is that. But it is also something intelligently contrived and carefully developed. Each element in it can be justified. Like the rest of the poem, the close is an exercise within limits.

V

It was Milton's explicit intention in *Paradise Lost* to argue, and this is not in any way a weakness in his art. Besides being a very eloquent and human poem, it is also an aggressively ideological one, and its intellectual scheme is very beautiful. To the various sorts of complexity—stylistic, verbal, metaphorical, mythical—that it has been recognized to have,[16] we should also add a complexity that is logical. If we ignore its argument (perhaps because we no longer believe in it), we make it a smaller and less subtle poem. In its time it stands as a great monument to what the mind can achieve. Milton after all wrote it with years of deliberation about its particular subject and its issues behind him. And, given his passion for literature as well as for morality and theology, it is also a literary critic's poem in the same way that Pope's poems are literary critic's poems. His blindness too necessarily made him a poet of intense inwardness and concentration. Shut up in the darkness of his physical world, he lived long and closely with his poem. It takes all the strain of his passion for right and conscious living, for justification, for logic and controversy. These were the powers of mind—and what a mind it was—that the poem irradiated:

> So much the rather thou Celestial light
> Shine inward, and the mind through all her powers
> Irradiate, there plant eyes, all mist from thence
> Purge and disperse, that I may see and tell
> Of things invisible to mortal sight.
>
> (III, 51-55)

[16] See for example: Stein, *Answerable Style;* MacCaffrey, *Paradise Lost as Myth;* Cope, *The Metaphoric Structure of Paradise Lost;* Christopher Ricks, *Milton's Grand Style* (Oxford, 1963).

# Index

Abdiel, 38
Achilles, 11
Adam, passim; see also Man; his freedom, 32-33; his relationship with Eve, 46-48, 78, 150-159, 163-177; his separation from Eve, 80-96; 'not deceav'd' at the Fall, 89-90, 159-162; his knowledge, 101-102, 104-123; his fall, 137-139, 145-146, 150-177, 193-197; instructed by Michael, 12, 187-201
*Adam in Ballingschap*, 82
*Adamo Caduto*, 52, 81, 160
*Adamus Exul*, 52, 126, 143 n., 160
Addison, Joseph, 18, 41, 198-199
Aeneas, 12, 30
Alfred, King, 16
Ames, William, 79
Angels, interest in Man, 26-27; can (like Man) be deceived, 100; their knowledge, 108-123; are (like Man) ignorant of God's secrets, 110-111; can (unlike Man) fly, 110-118; know (unlike Man) by intuition, 111-112; are (like Man) tried in obedience, 125; are (like Man) not corrupted by unapproved evil thoughts, 132; have (like Man) appetites of hunger, 135-136; and of sex, 158-159
Angels, fallen, 37, 58-60, 63, 147-149
Appetites, 127, 129-130, 132, 134-139, 144, 148, 190-197
Approval, in moral life, 84-85, 92-93, 116, 132, 155, 161-162
Aristotle, 11, 64, 95, 129-130, 191
Arnold, Matthew, 120

Arthur, King, 15-16
Astronomy, 109-110, 115-123
Atonement, the, 25-26, 35, 37, 197-198
Augustine, St, 65, 122

Bacon, Francis, 106-107, 111
Baker, Herschel, 2 n., 60 n.
Beasts, in Paradise, 49-56; and Man, 140, 176; sexual appetite in, 154-155, 175-176; after Fall, 182
Beaumont, Joseph, 81, 134 n.
Beelzebub, 38
Bell, Millicent, 80 n., 94, 129 n.
Bentley, Richard, 6, 199
Bible, passim; rationality of, 3-9; 17-20, 40; I Corinthians, 120, 152, 170, 172; II Corinthians, 189; Daniel, 29; Genesis, passim; Genesis, **chapter 1**, 44-45, 140, 150-156, 163; **chapter 2**, 7, 43, 44, 45, 46, 76, 83, 89, 102-103, 126, 150-156, 165, 166; **chapter 3**, 3, 7, 39, 46, 48, 53, 71, 76, 77, 89, 97, 101, 103, 124, 126, 128, 132, 133, 137, 140, 178, 181; **chapter 4**, 190; **chapter 6**, 193; **chapter 8**, 184-185; Hebrews, 26; Job, 20, 50, 110, 187; Jonah, 30; Joshua, 119; Jude, 26; Judges, 4; Matthew, 122, 169; II Peter, 23; Psalms, 134 n.; Revelation, 8-9, 23-24, 27, 53, 56; Romans, 184; I Timothy, 89, 159
Boethius, 65, 72
Bowra, C. M., 63 n.
Broadbent, J. B., 41 n.
Browne, Sir Thomas, 3-4, 97
Bunyan, John, 33